I0231850

BREAKING BONDAGES

LIFE CHANGING TESTIMONIES

MARIA ERIKSSON

BREAKING BONDAGES
Life-Changing Testimonies

© 2015 by Maria Eriksson
All rights reserved

A Master Press Cover Design

All Scripture quotations are from:
The Holy Bible, New King James Version (NKJV)
Copyright 1982 by Thomas Nelson, Inc.
Thomas Nelson Publishers. All Rights Reserved

Printed in the United States
ALL RIGHTS RESERVED

No part of this publication may be reproduced, stored in a retrieval system, or transmitted, in any form or by any means—electronic, mechanical, photocopying, recording, or otherwise—without written permission

BREAKING BONDAGES
Life-Changing Testimonies

ISBN 978-0-9913121-5-3
For information:

MASTER PRESS

3405 ISLAND BAY WAY, KNOXVILLE, TN 37931
Mail to: publishing@ masterpressbooks.com

BREAKING BONDAGES

LIFE-CHANGING TESTIMONIES

Maria Eriksson

DEDICATION

I am dedicating this book to my Lord Jesus who through these trials rescued me from the rotten mud where I used to live. I would also like to dedicate it to my brother Francisco, who had to suffer in order for me to come to learn the divine Truth. My conversion of faith was also possible through the pain of losing my mother and brother Martin in a short period of time. Last but not least, I am dedicating it to my blood-family and my brethren in Christ whom I love indeed.

ACKNOWLEDGMENT

I thank God for the undeserved (unmerited) gift of salvation. I thank Him for the guidance He has given me and granting me the inspiration to finish this work. Special thanks to my husband, my two daughters and two sons for their patience while I spent hours writing this book.

CONTENTS

Dedication 5

Acknowledgment 7

Introduction 11

Chapter 1. The New Life 13

Chapter 2. Trials Bring Us Closer to God 19

Chapter 3. My Greatest Disappointment 27

Chapter 4. The Despairing Cry 31

Chapter 5. Recovering the Lost Kingdom 43

Chapter 6. God Heals all Illness 49

Chapter 7. Persistence with Faith Moves God 55

Chapter 8. God Always Answers our Requests 63

Chapter 9. God Continues to Send Phillip(s) to Baptize People 67

Chapter 10. The False Teachers. 73

Chapter 11. God Speaks to Us in Various Forms 81

Chapter 12. God Opens and Closes Doors. 91

Chapter 13. Divine Revelations through Dreams 95

Chapter 14. Walking with God 111

Chapter 15. Our Best Teacher 117

Chapter 16. Doubts and Miracles 121

Chapter 17. We are in Bondage with The World 127

Chapter 18. Religion and Salvation: Two Different Things 133

Chapter 19. From Darkness to Light 139

Chapter 20. The Universal Commission 149

Chapter 21. Spirits of Religion 161

Chapter 22. The Spiritual Gifts and the Mistakes related to them . 167

Chapter 23. Selfishness and Its Consequences 177

Chapter 24. Prayer and Faith 181

Conclusion 185

INTRODUCTION

I am sure this might sound strange to you as much as it did to me when I hear the expression "We are in bondage". When I heard my dying mother telling me to cut her rope, which is a synonym of bondage I did not understand her. To be able to understand what bondage means it is necessary to seek God's guidance. This was one of the very first lessons God has taught me since the moment I sought Him. The Holy Spirit wants us to learn how to be free and how to set others free of bondage. The Bible states that we are captives of this world to do the devil's will, but we have a Savior who has already defeated the executioner. (2 Timothy 2:24-26). Through the Holy Scriptures we can find a number of testimonies of how God had spoken to people. God continues speaking to the beings He created in similar ways. There are thousands of books that narrate amazing testimonies of the way God has manifested to common people and mine is one of them. My prayer is that my testimonies will inspire you to open your heart to God and could receive the Holy Spirit to lead your life.

Chapter 1

The New Life

There was a man sent from God, whose name was John.
This man came for a witness, to bear witness of the Light,
that all men through him might believe. He was not that Light,
but was sent to bear witness of that Light. That was the true
Light that gives light to every man coming into the world.

John 1: 6-9

John the Baptist was sent to prepare the way of the Lord Jesus Christ for His first coming. All his disciples now have the mission of preparing the way for His second coming. I am trying to use the last drop of God's grace given to me to become a mature Christian to shine the Light of Jesus for others to learn the truth and be set free.

Someone once asked me why I had changed so radically. This was a Jewish relative who has known me for more than twenty years. He thought this change was strange. My answer was clear when I told him that I had found myself in a dark tunnel with no way out. I shared with him in full details all the tragedies my family in Mexico had suffered and he believed because he knows them. I pray to the Lord that with the help of the Holy Spirit, my testimonies can help transform him and come to know the truth as well. The pain and unbearable anguish I faced made me look for help and when I could not find it here among men I had to look from above. Jesus Christ said: *"Come to Me, all you who labor and are heavy laden, and I will give you rest"* (Matthew 11:28).

> *For He has not despised nor abhorred the affliction of the afflicted;*
> *Nor has He hidden His face from Him; But when He cried to Him,*
> *He heard.*
>
> Psalm 22: 24

The British writer, Clive Staples Lewis once said: "God whispers and speaks to the conscience through pleasures but He screams to the conscience through pain." Pain is a type of alarm that goes off to wake up a world that sleeps unaware of any danger. In other words, God is letting us know that in order to grow spiritually we need to suffer (Psalm 78:34-35). In the Bible we read that we should rejoice in time of suffering and trials because He will be with us and will help us get through them (James 1:2-3). Trials are difficult and obscure testing times, which lead us to think that God does not love us. Otherwise we would not be going through such ordeals. God is trying to bring us closer to Him but we cannot understand it due to our spiritual immaturity. He wants to sanctify and purify our spirits to start a close relationship. In God's sight we are like gold. We are like the precious metal that must be tested by fire to see its real beauty and purity. Suffering is one of the tools God uses to purify us and help us grow.

Through suffering and pain when we are tested with fire as if we were gold, our soul is cleansed and healed; and our spirit strengthened. The Holy Spirit took Jesus Christ to the desert right after His baptism to test Him. He spent forty days living among wild beasts without food or water. God the Father gave Him this test to prepare Him to defeat the devil and save the world. The Holy Scriptures tell that He did not eat or drink water during the entire time in the desert. I think He could not even sleep knowing that wild animals were surrounding Him, besides the lack of food and water. I can testify that when we fast for days it is difficult to fall asleep. God, the Father sustained Him to be able to pass this incredible test. The

The New Life   15

same happens to all of us; God sustains and helps us to pass any trial or to overcome any difficulty if we truly trust Him with all our heart. We cannot pass the tests given by the Lord without His support. If we do not pass it we have to repeat the same test for as long as it is necessary. Perhaps we might have to wander in circles as the Israelites did in the desert and never come to the resting place that God has designed for us. Remember, He has promised to answer prayers as long as we seek Him with a humble heart.

The Lord will strengthen him on his bed of illness;
You will sustain him on his sickbed.
Psalm 41: 3

Indeed, I received the answer to my suffering from above. As soon as I called upon the Lord, He came to my rescue and comforted me with words of hope and faith. The peace of God came in the mist of the storm and strengthened me to bare the difficulties, which brought me closer to Him. Ever since then, I understood that life without God is meaningless; frankly it does not even exist. The Spirit of God gives us life. We are dead without Christ. The Bible states that He is the way, the truth, and the life. No one comes to the Father but through Him (John 14: 6, 16). God is always calling us to share His life with us as the Holy Scriptures say: "Behold, I stand at the door and knock. If anyone hears My voice and opens the door, I will come in to him and dine with him, and he with Me." (Revelation 3:20). The door of our heart can only be open from inside; therefore, we have to let Him in. No one can come in unless we open the door for them, and that includes the Holy Spirit of God. God being almighty could open the door and let Himself in but He would not do it. He is a gentleman who has provided us with free-will when He made us. We must choose between opening and not opening the door when He knocks.

God is continually calling us but our sin is a barrier that alienates us from Him. Through His prophets God revealed it to us:

Behold, the Lord's hand is not shortened, That it cannot save;
Nor His ear heavy, That it cannot hear.
But your iniquities have separated you from your God;
And your sins have hidden His face from you, So that He will not hear.

Isaiah 59: 1-2

When we approach the Lord with a humble heart repenting from all our wrongdoing, He forgives us. The barrier of sin that stood between God and us breaks and our supplications ascends to Him immediately. Then, we start feeling a fresh anointing like a gentle breeze sent by Him, which cleanses us from our impurity. This flow of a fresh anointing liberates us from any burden. His forgiveness comes through our faith in Jesus Christ. How great is our God!

Jesus pours out the Holy Spirit upon us to protect us every day and to help us communicate with Him. The Holy Spirit is like a bell that rings when we do something wrong. We must remain alert praying and asking for forgiveness for our wrong thoughts and deeds every time we feel convicted. Through our continued prayers, we keep our communication channel wide open. Without the interference of sin, we can listen to God's voice telling us of any troubles along the way. If we stay off task we fall into the Devil's schemes. He is always trying to confuse us and to discourage us. He throws at us vain ideas that go against God's commandments and will. If we do not pray or do the things God has commanded us to do in his Holy Scriptures, we will slowly start departing from Him. Our mind and thoughts will become dull. As time passes, we become familiar with this sounding bell, which warns us from danger and alerts us from our wrongdoing. Its sound does not even bother us. We simply ignore it. God does not want anybody to go to hell. He will continue calling us and He might use different and unimaginable methods to get our attention. This is the love He has for all of us! God desires for us to live our new life near Him. He longs to be with us, to have a relationship with us just as two who love each other long to be together.

Words That Bring Life

Just like the majority of people, I thought I had won my salvation by attending church every Sunday. I thought if I kept a few religious rituals and did not commit the deadly sins, I would be saved. I was very wrong and never thought about what Jesus Christ did on the cross for me. It is very common to hear people say; "I'm a good person" "I do no harm to anyone; therefore I deserve to go to heaven. I too would compare myself with others that would do crazier things than I would. Since I did not do the things they did, I thought I was walking with God.

People do not go to heaven because they are good. In one of my visits to a convalescent home, I met a lady who showed a great interest in the Gospel. She asked me to come back soon to keep talking about Jesus Christ. I returned two days later. She listened carefully as I narrated the testimony of my conversion. Before I left I asked her if she wanted to invite Jesus into her heart and experience what I had experienced. She answered yes and we both prayed together. While I led her in prayer, I asked God to forgive her sins. She stopped praying and looked at me with rage and refused to ask God for forgiveness. When I saw her reaction, I remembered what she had shared with me the first day we met. She had mentioned her frustration when people would tell her that the reason she was sick and in the convalescent home was because God was punishing her. She also mentioned her anger toward God for taking her health away and for not being able to use her legs. She was in a wheelchair; she wanted to run marathons. She continued saying that she did not believe them because she was a good person and had never offended God. Based on her standards she did not have to ask God to forgive her. I was convicted to tell her that God had allowed her to be ill to slow her down from the daily routine and have a chance to speak with her.

The reaction of that person when I asked God to forgive her troubled me. I stopped praying aloud and silently begged to the Lord to support me to continue sharing the truth with that lady. God listened to my prayer request and quickly came to my assistance. He reminded me about the Lord's Prayer and how to use it to bring that lady back on track. The Holy Spirit led me step by step until that person recognized that she was a sinner. I asked her

18   Breaking Bondages

if she knew the Lord's Prayer and she started to recite it fast and clear. I reminded her that Jesus taught His disciples how to pray by using that prayer, and explained to her that God wants us to pray not to recite memorized words. In other words I told her she needed to slow down and reflect upon the things she was requesting from the Heavenly Father. Together we started to analyze word by word. When we arrived to the part where it says that we need His forgiveness as we forgive others, I told her to stop, and she did it. I asked her if she really had forgiven every person who had offended her. She looked at me startled while the question convicted her of being a liar. She then said no, I have not forgiven every one. There came another question. Who are you speaking to and to whom are you lying every time you recite this prayer? She looked at me again and then she responded to the question in a sad way and said to God. She expressed that she did not want to remain lying to our Lord in heaven.

Once that woman received the first conviction of sin, I suggested to her to change that part of the Lord's Prayer where she was lying. I recommended she make that part of the prayer into a request for help to forgive her offenders. After that question I made a series of questions based on the Ten Commandments and finally she acknowledged she was disobeying most of them. In her own words she recognized she was a liar, thief, idolater and more. I explained to her using the Holy Scriptures that God was going to punish her up to the fourth generation if she did not love and keep God's commandments (Exodus 20:5). The next question got to the bottom of her heart and pushed her to seek for God's mercy. Where do you think you would go if you died at this moment without repentance and forgiveness? She responded sadly and said to hell but I do not want to go there. Immediately she said I want to be forgiven and cleansed from head to toe. Together we prayed and I led her to invite Jesus into her heart, which she received with tears in her eyes. The word of God which is living and active, sharper than a double edged sword penetrated her soul and helped her to see that she was dead in sin (Hebrews 4:12). It is amazing the way our Lord works to rescue His lost sheep.

Chapter 2

Trials Bring Us Closer to God

In this you greatly rejoice, though now for a little while, if need be, you have been grieved by various trials, that the genuineness of your faith, being much more precious than gold that perishes, though it is tested by fire, may be found to praise, honor, and glory at the revelation of Jesus Christ,

1 Peter 1:6-7

God desires everybody to be saved. In order to purify and save us, He allows us to endure difficult trials. Through this dark season of hardships we are experiencing, we reflect and come to the conclusion only God can help us to find the solution. Then we approach Him with a desperate cry. People have asked me how I met God. Every time people ask me this question my answer is this: I thought I have known Him since my childhood but now I realize that it was not true. To "know" someone means to be "close" to that person. I met God in my adult life though I must admit that He was always there for me.

20   Breaking Bondages

I met the Lord at a hospital in Guadalajara by the bedside of my brother. My brother laid in a coma caused by an MRI to detect a fistula in the brain area. He was my younger brother but I loved him as if he were my own child. My heart ached to see him helpless with tubes everywhere. I was despondent and wanted desperately to be able to help him. I stood by his bedside watching him and keeping him clean. From time to time I would wet his mouth and tongue to refresh him. He had been in a coma for two days before I got to the hospital. I spent the day near him and at night I had to leave the hospital for only one person could stay with him. My brothers thought I could not help. At the hospital they preferred a man who could help move him if necessary. In that instance, I went to Michoacán to see my mom whom I had not seen for two years.

I traveled to Mexico to see my brother because I knew it would be the last time I would see him alive. I also went over to meet my Savior, Jesus Christ, but that I did not know. Two days later I returned to Guadalajara along with my mother, father and a sister. We took turns at the hospital to see my sick brother. In the same room was another ill man in bed and his wife was with him. While my mother was visiting my brother the lady who was accompanying her husband prayed with her. She saw my mom reciting words that were not helping my brother because nothing changed. The word of God says: "And when you pray, do not use vain repetitions as the heathen *do*. For they think that they will be heard for their many words" (Matt. 6: 7).

The lady offered to pray for my brother because she had faith that her prayers would be heard. When my mother returned to the hospital waiting room she told me that a lady had prayed beautifully for my brother. My sister strongly objected to this. When my sister said that, it made me angry because nothing mattered to me more than my brother's recovery. I replied that if that prayer would benefit my brother I did not care who said it. Thank God my brother's wellbeing was more important to me than my own religion. When my turn came to be with my brother in the room, I stood next to him and took his hand. I also made repetitious prayers as it was all I knew. I prayed the Lord's Prayer and Psalm 23 because I knew them by heart. I cried because in the bottom of my heart I desired that my prayers were received and a miracle would occur.

The same lady who had prayed earlier offered to pray with me as well. Her husband suffered from multiple sclerosis. He was receiving treatment that would restore strength to his muscles temporarily. When she saw that I was praying like my mother, she felt sorry for me. I gladly accepted her offer and we began to pray together. I immediately felt peace and somehow I sensed that I was speaking directly with God. I expressed to Him my desires with all my heart. From that moment I began to have faith. My parents had to return to Michoacán that afternoon. Before leaving, they noticed my brother was opening his eyes a little and he seemed to have a small improvement.

Before leaving the hospital, my dad asked a Catholic chaplain to administer the last rites to my brother. He thought that my brother would die soon. The last rites are a ritual where the priest anoints the sick with oil on the forehead as he recites a prayer. The Apostle James said, "Is anyone among you sick? Let him call for the elders of the church, and let them pray over him, anointing him with oil in the name of the Lord" (James 5:14). The elders of the church are holy people who consecrate their life to God, have a strong relationship with the Lord. They are not just religious people. The Holy Spirit is the one who gives us power to heal the sick. The person applying the oil must be full of it and have an extraordinary faith. If the person applying the oil has no faith then what he/she does has no power. I know by experience that in Catholicism we do not have a close relationship with God. We are always praying to the statues of different people who according to Catholic tradition are saints. How can we expect a miracle from God if we are disobeying his commandments and do not know how to pray?

After my parents left, the lady and I prayed more. The Bible says: Again I say to you that if two of you agree on earth concerning anything that they ask, it will be done for them by My Father in heaven. For where two or three are gathered together in My name, I am there in the midst of them" (Matthew 18:19-20). It does not say that He will give us what we ask in Mary's, John's, or any other name. With this promise in mind we joined our prayers for the rapid recovery of my brother. The illness of my brother brought me closer to God.

The first miracle

My parents left me sadder than I was before. I stood by my brother fervently praying and believing that only a miracle could lift him up from that bed. At around ten p.m. I was told to leave the room for visiting time was over. Another brother was going to stay with him. Before leaving for the hotel room, I asked the lady again if we could pray once more for my brother. When her husband heard me say that, he offered to pray too. He said that his wife prays beautifully but he wanted to lead us now. Gladly I asked him to please do so. He got up with the help of an orthopedic device so we joined our hands together in prayer around my brother's bed. This gentleman prayed more earnestly assured that a miracle would happen there.

It was amazing to hear people talking to God directly from the heart without vain repetitions. When we were praying with our eyes closed, I felt as if a light had illuminated the room and my brother. I felt a sense of relief and joy that was difficult to hide. As I walked back to the hotel with my older brother I expressed to him that a miracle has taken place that night in our brother's hospital room. My excitement seemed to bother him as he told me that he did not like to speak about God. I had to silence my joy for the moment but once in my room I thanked God for giving me the faith I had. I could not sleep for hours due to the emotional upheaval of the day. At about five in the morning we were told that my brother was out of the coma. He was speaking as if nothing had happened to him. That was the best news I had heard in my life.

I literally ran back to the Hospital to see the miracle first hand. I hugged and kissed him like crazy for I could not hide my emotions. I told my brother that his recovery was due to the prayers we had done with the nice people next to his bed. I learned that my brother woke up and removed the tubes from his mouth and nose approximately ten minutes after I left. Immediately after we fervently prayed, a miracle happened visible for patients, doctors and nurses in the hospital room. From that moment my faith grew tremendously. I just wanted to be near my brother. I could not believe what my eyes saw. I asked the nurses to feed him, but the doctors were taking many

Trials Bring Us Closer to God   23

precautions. They did not want to feed him yet.

The doctors and nurses were speaking about the miracle that happened. My brother woke up very hungry and thirsty. He was always a good eater! The moment I learned about this miracle I wanted to shout from the rooftops that Jesus Christ exists, is alive and does amazing miracles. I felt like a child with a new toy. I went from room to room visiting the sick and speaking of what had happened to my brother. I wanted to share my faith with them so they could receive the benefits it brings. I know that several people believed.

My brother had to stay in bed for some time for observation, but he seemed happy. He did not recognize me until the next day. He did not see me for more than two years and did not expect to see me there. He would tell me "I do not know you madam but I have great faith in you". I think that he said that because he might have heard my prayers while he was in the coma. He left the hospital three days after he awoke from the coma. I returned to my home, and he went back to Michoacán confident that he had already been healed.

The man who had prayed for my brother was discharged from the hospital a day after the miracle. Before he left he gave me a book that teaches how to pray. He said that we need to say with faith that my brother had been healed by the stripes of our Lord Jesus Christ. Before I left I told my brother to decree that promise in faith. Then, I called my brother almost every day and asked if he kept saying the phrase that gave honor and glory to our Lord Jesus Christ for his recovery. He assured me that he was doing it every day. Now that I know more about the Word of God I can discern the true meaning of the Bible verse: "But He was wounded for our transgressions, He was bruised for our iniquities; The chastisement for our peace was upon Him, And by His stripes we are healed" (Isaiah 53: 5). That phrase should be placed in our hearts and spoken with our lips for healing of body and spirit. It speaks of the ultimate sacrifice of Jesus on the cross of Calvary that we might have eternal life. The Lord healed my brother's spirit as he died peacefully.

Peace during the trial

*These things I have spoken to you, that in Me you may have peace. In the
world you will have tribulation; but be of good cheer,
I have overcome the world.*

John 16:33

I returned home happy sharing with everyone about the miracle God
performed for my brother. I was sure he would be fine, but my Heavenly
Father had other plans. My brother only lived for two months after the miracle
occurred. When I went to his funeral something really strange happened to
me. As I approached the coffin to see his face, I clearly felt someone touching
my shoulder. I heard a whispering voice telling me not to cry because he
was in a better place. When I saw my brother's face, he seemed to smile. An
inexplicable peace comforted me there at the time. Rather than to mourn I
apologized to him for not letting him go. I felt remorse because I prayed to
God for healing not minding His will or that of my brother. Later the Lord
showed me through a dream how my brother rose from his coffin when I
approached him to see his dead body. The Bible speaks of the promise of
salvation made by God to His disciples. *"For* the promise is to you and to your
children, and to all who are afar off, as many as the Lord our God will call"
(Acts 2:39).

The Word of God is truthful. My mom's only desire was salvation for her
child. Our Heavenly Father will not give us anything worse because we are
his children as the Bible states it in the following verse: "If you then, being
evil, know how to give good gifts to your children, how much more will your
Father who is in heaven give good things to those who ask Him!" (Matthew
7:11). My brother had a sad life. He was forced to move away from his wife
and children for mistakes he made in the past. His wife refused to move
back to Mexico and divorced him. My mother prayed that he never remarry
since he was married by the church. For if he had married again it would be
committing adultery. It was very difficult for him to live alone; he was young

Trials Bring Us Closer to God   25

and handsome. God took him at the right time assuring his salvation.

We must be careful what we ask of our eternal Father. I say this because for a young man who has had a woman it is almost impossible not to be with another. Our heavenly Father listened to our prayers, and He responded to my mom's request. He always decides what is best for us even though sometimes it is hard to believe and accept everything. The Lord gave my brother time to repent of his sins and gave him faith in Jesus Christ. In the scriptures we can see that that is all we need to be saved. "…that if you confess with your mouth the Lord Jesus and believe in your heart that God has raised Him from the dead, you will be saved" (Romans 10:9).

My brother believed in God's Word before he died. He told me that he proclaimed the following verse every day: *"for the wounds of my Lord Jesus Christ I am healed."* My brother's faith was not in me as I mentioned it before, but in God our Lord. He just believed that the miracle had happened by my faith in God and not by his. In other words he was sure God would give me what I ask. He knew my greatest desire at the time was for him to regain his health. To God the physical body's health is not as important as the health of the spirit. I've come to know this through reading the Scriptures and constant prayer. The body that we lose on earth God is going to replace it with a glorified one that will never corrupt. The Bible says "Behold, I tell you a mystery: We shall not all sleep, but we shall all be changed— in a moment, in the twinkling of an eye, at the last trumpet. For the trumpet will sound, and the dead will be raised incorruptible, and we shall be changed. For this corruptible must put on incorruption, and this mortal *must* put on immortality" (1 Corinthians 15:51-53). A year later these promises brought peace to my heart. Now I hope to re-join with my loved ones one day in paradise.

Chapter 3

My Greatest Deception

And we know that all things work together for good to those
who love God, to those who are the called according to His purpose.

Romans 8:28

After my brother's death I lost all my faith in God. Based on my ignorance, I thought God did not exist. He started a miracle and left it half way done? It could not be God. We need to know God to understand His ways. My assumptions were based solely on traditions. According to God's Word, to cure also means to save one's spirit. Let's take a look at what the scriptures have to say about this: "Then behold, they brought to Him a paralytic lying on a bed. When Jesus saw their faith, He said to the paralytic, "Son, be of good cheer; your sins are forgiven you" (Matthew 9:2). Even though they had asked for health for the body, God gave them that and something much more valuable as the spiritual health. He has abundance to give us. My brother died on November eleventh, the same day my mother and my twin brother and sister were born. One month after my brother's death my mother started to feel sick. Three months after my brother's death my mother was diagnosed with a cancerous tumor on her stomach. To find out that my mother was sick was devastating. Another

28   Breaking Bondages

pain to heap on top of what I was already suffering. It felt as if I was living a nightmare. I behaved like a zombie without knowing what to say or do. I did not hope for my mother to be healed. I would just cry day and night. I would go to work without knowing exactly what I was doing and sometimes I wouldn't even eat. I would spend my time making phone calls to Mexico to hear my mother's voice the most I could.

Upon receiving the news about my mom, I went to my church to request prayers. I asked the priest to add my mother's name to the list of the sick. I did this without faith, trying to follow my religion. Through my despair I noticed the way in which the prayer requests were presented in the mass. The list of names was read without giving any prayer. I left that church very discouraged thinking that there might be a better way. It is necessary to pray fervently to our heavenly Father in the name Jesus Christ. We must express our desires and needs with faith if we expect to receive an answer. The prayers must be humble, corroborating to God that His will is above everything we ask for. I shared my problems with a co-worker who was Christian. She listened to me but did not say anything. She did not know if I believed in God; therefore, she was afraid of my reaction. The next day I saw her; I knew it wasn't a coincidence. She expressed her feelings towards my situation and wanted to share her faith with me. The Lord Almighty had placed her in my path so that I could recover the faith I had lost.

My co-worker shared a testimony that convinced me to believe in miracles. Her father recovered from a stomach cancer similar to the one my mother had. The doctors had told him that there was no cure. While she was at church praying, her father in the hospital suddenly felt a whirlpool and a blow in his stomach. After that weird sense in his stomach he regained energy and went home happy. Her father was miraculously cured and lived for twenty-three more years. This testimony changed my life as it helped me believe in God. The devil got angry and set a trap for me to fall again. He tried very hard to keep me away from God.

My co-worker invited me to her church because they were going to have a prodigious preacher. They were informed that he supposedly possessed many spiritual gifts including healing the sick. On Saturday I got ready early and was the first one to arrive at the church. I wished with all my heart for a miracle to happen in my mother's life and get cured. It was not a good idea to attend that church. That night I was very disappointed. The guest preacher turned out to be a liar that only came to deceive the innocent believers. I left through the back door of the building where this small congregation was meeting. I did not have the money he asked for to pay for the miracle. I just left crying about my miserable life. After that meeting, my co-worker avoided me because she was ashamed. She did not know who the preacher really was and had also been misled. She was distressed due to the fact that I had seen this absurdity in her church. I continued going to the Catholic Church every Sunday as I had always done. Listening to the same memorized rituals in that church did not give me any relief, but it was my custom. I was convinced that if my church was not helping me, neither would any other. I had never seen such deceit. Mainly where you think the spiritual leaders are to assist us in times of trouble.

Now I have learned that there are false prophets and teachers of the Word everywhere. The devil can disguise as an angel of light to try to deceive people (2 Peter. 2:1-2). Nowadays, many people are deceived by religious leaders. They interpret the Word of God according to their own beliefs and interests. These teachers speak sugarcoated words that bring lots of people to their congregations. The prosperity doctrines are very attractive to people especially now in times of financial crisis. People are giving all their savings to those wolves that the only thing they care about is themselves. This has been written as one of the signals of the end times. Only those who follow Jesus are free of those fabrications because they have the light that guides them always. Man can deceive us but God would never do it. He allowed me to go through more suffering in order to grab my attention. It is amazing to feel God's presence during the trials. When our Heavenly Father is calling us, He gives a little blow and if we do not listen He hits us with a hammer and if we still continue to ignore him, He hits us with a sledgehammer. I believe that after those tough hits, He leaves us alone with our ignorance. He is just trying to open our eyes so we can choose if we want to follow him. He lets us choose between eternal life in His presence or eternal condemnation away from Him.

If we reject God we will suffer for the eternity the atrocious torments in hell. Hell is discussed throughout the Bible, but many people prefer to ignore it. God wants to prevent people from going to that horrible place which is the final abode of those who disobey Christ. I am now asking God to forgive me for my ignorance. I am infinitely thankful for His mercy that caught my attention. Thanks to the hurtful beatings, today I can say that my mother and brother are saved. I am confident that one day I shall be reunited with them both. The great disappointments caused by my spiritual leaders have taught me an important lesson. The lesson learned is that I should never trust in men. The only faithful one is Jesus and He is the light that will lead us all the way to heaven (John 8:12).

Chapter 4

The Despairing Cry

Thus says the LORD:
"Cursed is the man who trusts in man
And makes flesh his strength,
Whose heart departs from the LORD..."
Jeremiah 17:5

The trials continued with more intensity. Two weeks after the great disappointment at my friend's congregation, I received once again terrible news. One of my youngest brothers was kidnapped. Some men had blocked the road and didn't let him go through. With lies, they told him to get out of his car and then forced him to get in another vehicle. They left his wife, son and mother-in-law scared and crying on a solitary road. This sad news came in the worse of the times. It had only been a few months after my brother's death, my mother was very sick and as if this wasn't enough now another brother was missing. At that time my first reaction was to go to church and ask the priest to pray for my family. The priest showed concern for my family and told me he would do it. Next Sunday when I returned to church I noticed that the name of my brother was not in the list of prayer requests. Days passed and the family was desperate without any encouraging news. They looked for him everywhere. When they would hear that there were dead people found in some place they would immediately investigate to see if it was him.

My despair continued to grow with every passing minute. Another week went by. I went to church as I accustomed to do every Sunday. I expected to hear my brother's name mentioned. I was trying to get some hope or at least some pity. My distress grew even more when once again I didn't hear his name. The priest read the names of people who were sick and also people already deceased. When church was over my husband and I approached the priest and asked him why he didn't pray for my brother? I couldn't believe the answer the priest gave us. He said that his ceremony does not have a category to pray for the kidnapped. His answer felt worse than having a bucket of cold water splashed on me on a winter day. That answer would have puzzled anyone, but in my situation, it was cruel. I went home very disappointed. I locked myself in my room and cried day and night without any hope. Two churches had denied me any support in a period of drastic need.

I was in a tunnel that grew longer and darker day by day. Seeing this in retrospect, I feel sorry for that priest. What a great ignorance exists in some churches. To speak with our Father in heaven we do not need ceremonies or categorized petitions. All we need is to express our feelings to God from the bottom of our heart. I did not know this and I was trusting in man. Finally, in the solitude of my room with my shattered soul I spoke to the Being that created the universe and everything in it. I told Him that there was not anyone that could help me to escape from that dark tunnel. I challenged Him to show me that He exists and hears our requests. I promised that I would make certain sacrifices until He proved to me that He was alive. My request was that if my brother was already dead, that we could find his body to stop looking for him. In my ignorance I added with some sarcasm: "I am not asking you for something impossible." As if there were some impossible things for Him. He had to show me He was hearing my prayers and had to give me an answer. I also promised Him that if He granted me my request I would live eternally grateful. I was going to spend the rest of my life giving praise and thanks to Him.

The days would go by and we were not receiving any news about my brother. No one was asking for ransom. My desperation led me to look for spiritual help. I looked for help in congregations with different doctrines. God was already at work in the restoration of my faith. From the moment I realized that God is the only one that could help us, He came to my rescue. He started to guide me and showed me how to read the Holy Scriptures. Little by little I learned to know our Lord God. I would drive to work every day talking to Him. I know that the following thing I did would sound crazy, but it's written that we would be judged like that. I would vacate the passenger seat to God so He could be my partner. During my journey on the road I talked to Him and started to feel His presence. Even in the midst of the storm I could feel peace. He would comfort me and that was the only way I was able to go forth while I waited for a miracle to happen. I began to thank Him in advance for that miracle I was waiting to receive. His Holy Spirit was guiding me to do His will. The Holy Scriptures show that we must be thankful for all that we are and everything we have and even to what He is yet to give us. God has an immense abundance of blessings for those of us who decide to pick up our cross and walk with him.

I asked my co-worker if she could pray for my family with her congregation. This time I told her that my problems were duplicated. Not only was I suffering from my brother's death, a mother suffering with terminal cancer but now I had a missing brother who was in the hands of dangerous criminals. These Christian people gathered every day to pray without ceasing. Being near people with faith in God strengthened my faith. I was on the verge of insanity and I couldn't even imagine how my mother was feeling. My friend invited many of the church members to her home to pray every night. We prayed and fasted for my brother's safe and healthy return. They had a huge faith that my brother would be set free.

Meanwhile in Mexico my poor mother forgot about her sickness to dedicate herself entirely to sacrifice and prayer. Nothing mattered to her except her son. She expressed to us her desire of walking on her knees throughout the streets in exchange for a miracle. The people in her town avoided her. They could not stand to see so much suffering in one person. In the course of three weeks my mother aged tremendously. She lost so much weight which made her look twenty years older. I felt so sad when I saw her.

She used to be a very strong woman, who did not cry when her son was buried. She just recited restlessly her rosaries and other memorized prayers she learned from her religion. She thought that her idols would be helping her in such moments.

Many people prayed for my brother's safe return but their prayers were different from ours. The Bible states that we do not receive because we do not know how to ask (James 4:3). I would pray to the heavenly Father in the name of His son Jesus Christ. Jesus said: "And whatever you ask in My name, that I will do, that the Father may be glorified in the Son" (John 14:13). My family, relatives, and acquaintances prayed to their "saints" and the Guadalupe Virgin. They worship their idols turning on candles and bringing floral arrangements. They made promises to them that they would go to visit their images and statues in different parts of the country. Within their despair and ignorance, my family would go from a seer or sorcerer to another. The sorcerers would make them do satanic rituals and pagan practices with which were greatly offending our Father. We all knew that as the days passed our hopes of finding my brother alive were fading. During that time there were many kidnappings in the country. Bodies used to appear everywhere hanging from bridges and trees. In the news we watched that beheaded bodies were found everywhere. Sometimes they would even throw people alive to the tigers to be devoured.

I regained my faith in Jesus Christ thanks to the saints who God placed in my way. I say saints because that is how the Bible calls to the followers of Jesus Christ. Saint just means that we are separated for God. If you are dedicating your life to God's service; then you are a saint. My friend would ask me every day if there were any news of my brother just to hear the same sad answer. She would always urge me to believe the promises of God. She would assure me that my brother would be back alive and I would believe her. Her prayers always comforted me. We would ask God our Father to send His Holy Spirit and His angels to protect my brother. I called my family requesting they stop consulting the sorcerers. I had learned that God hates those things as the Scriptures would say. "There shall not be found among you *anyone* who makes his son or his daughter pass through the fire, *or one* who practices witchcraft, *or* a soothsayer, or one who interprets omens, or a sorcerer, or one who conjures spells, or a medium, or a spiritualist, or one who calls up the dead. For all who do these things *are* an abomination to the Lord, and because of these abominations the Lord your God drives them out from before you" (Deuteronomy 18: 10-12).

"The fear of the Lord is the beginning of wisdom;" (Psalm 111:10). The Lord transformed my heart quickly. I just wanted to please God so that He would protect my brother. My family, in desperation, continued to visit the occultists and even invoked Satan for help. One of my brothers said that he would receive the help from anyone including the devil. Meanwhile they sank in their ignorance; the Lord Almighty kept increasing my faith little by little. My heavenly Father guided my journey. The whole family was very scared and I did not know what to do. Rumors were heard that the whole family was in danger. They wanted to move away but did not know where to go with a very ill mother. I decided to go to Mexico to be with my mom during that harsh season. My husband and children opposed the idea because they feared for my safety. There was great tension among the family, but with God's blessing I was able to spread my faith to everyone.

My brother's release

A phone call early in the morning before my departure to Mexico woke me up. My oldest brother was informing us that my brother had appeared. With the shuttered voice I asked if he was fine. He said that my brother was alive. He was half dead with his ears hanging from a side, bruised and dehydrated but still alive. That incredible news filled my heart with joy. As soon as I heard his answer I knelt on the floor and gave thanks to God for this great prodigy. At that moment it felt as if someone had taken a very heavy burden off of me. I had promised the heavenly Father that I would be eternally thankful to Him for the rest of my life. There were no words to express my gratitude to God. My husband suffered along with me. My suffering disturbed him as well. He offered some tremendous sacrifices in my support. After hearing the news he said, "No more casinos". We both enjoyed visiting casinos. Most of our vacations were planned to places with casinos around.

God wants us to be free. All the addictions are traps set by the devil to keep us away from God. I did not consider myself an addict because I could control the money I would gamble. Honestly that was becoming harder every time I was in the casinos. For the second time, God was confirming His desire to keep me away from those addictive places. The first time was when I was informed that my brother was in coma. That morning we were ready to go to Las Vegas but instead, I went to Guadalajara. My reaction when I heard my husband say that we will not go to casinos any more was of unbelief. Then I thought he made the promise. I could go on my own without him because he could not fail to keep his promise. God convicted me immediately telling me that I had to support my husband who offered that to help my own family. I am partnering up with my husband on his sacrifice because God our heavenly Father deserves that and much more. Thank God we have not set a foot in a casino for more than seven years already and hopefully never will again.

During the time my brother was missing, my family and I forgot about my mother's disease. We were concentrating on one pain, the harder one. I imagined my brother being tortured and left without eating or drinking for more than three weeks. The morning they called me I was informed also that a huge amount of money was required for his rescue. I was told to bring to Mexico ten thousand dollars that day. The other part was going to be paid by the rest of the family. Although we did not have the required sum of money I was not disturbed by that. My brother was alive and that was most important. With the help of God, in the afternoon I was able to finish gathering some of the money and with that I went to Mexico to meet my family.

Before leaving to Mexico I asked my Christian friends to bless me. They blessed me and promised me to keep praying for my safe return. My brother wanted to see me as soon as I got to the town. He could barely walk due to the tortures he had endured. My emotions betrayed me when I saw him walking slowly towards me. It was a living miracle in front of my eyes. He was very afraid for he knew that he was not free yet from his captors. He was released under an oath in which he would meet up with them in three days. He had to present himself to a determined place to pay for the ransom. We gathered the money but he did not trust them. He thought that they would kill him as soon as they had received their money. He did not have any other option but to meet with them wherever and whenever they said. Had he not agreed to their conditions, the whole family would have to pay the consequences. Uncertainty had us all tormented but thanks to our Lord Jesus Christ all went well. The Lord Almighty was always with us sustaining us in the hardest of times.

My faith brought peace to my family. Everybody wanted to be near me because they felt safe. I inspired them to believe. I spoke to my brother about God's Word and made him read some Psalms. I anointed his head and feet with oil and together we sang praises to God. We went to church because he wanted to confess his sins to the priest and have him blessed as is customary in the Catholic religion. The priest, without the slightest remorse, responded that he did not have any time to do that. He was very indifferent towards my brother's situation and fears. He preferred to stay away from my brother. My brother left the church extremely disappointed at his spiritual leader. God was showing me for the second time that the doctrine I practiced is very wrong. God loves and cares for us and his servants should be likewise. Meanwhile, the captors were following my brother everywhere he went. He would not recognize them because he had his eyes covered. They were calling and threatening him day and night.

Six long days passed before his kidnappers summoned him to collect the money agreed. They extended the time agreed to exasperate us more. While waiting for them to summon him the whole family was united praying and singing hymns to God. Besides praying, I would fast and read the scriptures aloud to them because in the Word of God we would find peace. When they finally summoned him, He said goodbye crying and uttering that they would kill him. My mother, sister and I gathered to pray incessantly until he was free and gave us a call. I struggled because they insisted on reciting their repetitive prayers such as the rosary of liberation and who knows what other things that displease God (Mat. 6:7-8). My brother went from one site to another for six endless hours. If there was another car around the place where they were sending him, they would move to a different one. The criminals were afraid that they would be exposed and arrested. Besides the money my brother took newspapers to show them that he did not fail to his promise. He was very grateful that they released him. It was not them; it was God who made a way where there was none.

The storms settled for a while, but my trials were going to continue soon. I stayed in Mexico a few more days to take care of my mom since she was approaching her end. She made a huge effort to accompany me to the airport for my return to the US. I said goodbye to her crying because I felt that it was our farewell. After crossing the security checkpoint I turned my head to see her one more time. At that moment with tears in my eyes I asked my Lord Jesus Christ to take care of her. I pleaded to Him to allow me see her again. He surely gave me that wish. Two weeks before my mom died, the Lord sent me back to Mexico. God never forgets about our pleas even though we forget to thank Him for granting us our desires.

The horrors of the Kidnapping

Kidnapping is one of the worst experiences that a human being could suffer. I never imagined that one day I would experience such tribulation. I already had so much pain in my life to be able to bear something even more drastic. Now I know that God does not give us trials we cannot withstand as expressed by the Apostle Paul: "No temptation has overtaken you except such as is common to man; but God *is* faithful, who will not allow you to be tempted beyond what you are able, but with the temptation will also make the way of escape, that you may be able to bear *it*" (1 Corinthians 10:13). The terrible news came to me by my poor mother. It felt as if someone stabbed me in the heart, I cannot imagine how painful that was for her. I would have preferred to hide this news from her. She was suffering the recent loss of one son, the aching stomach cancer and now the kidnapping of another son. My brother's cavalry was also the family's cavalry.

He was missing for twenty-three days which each of those days seemed like twenty-three months. While we were unsuccessfully looking for him everywhere, he was being brutally tortured somewhere in the world. He was beaten without pity with hands and feet tied and his eyes covered. He was left without food or water for days. The mosquitoes and other insects were feasting on him while he was unable to defend himself. He shared with us that there were three instances in which he was almost executed. They tried to electrocute him once. His executioners flooded the room in which my brother was laying. They were about to put the electric shock into the water when they were interrupted by a phone call. Every time they were ready to execute him a phone call would prevent them from proceeding. He would also hear the tigers' roars and would listen as the tigers devoured the people that were thrown at them. He had been threatened to suffer the same death. Just imagining being devoured by beasts was enough for him to die of fright on top of all the tortures he was suffering. He begged them to grant him a favor. He asked his executors to throw his body somewhere where he could be found by his family. That was the same request I asked from God. I wanted to bury my brother to resume taking care of my mom until she also died. I find it curious that the kidnappers used to ask him to whom he prayed. Some expressed that they had never seen so many obstacles when trying to get rid of a miserable captive.

The tragedy had a happy ending. I narrated this tragedy, because it is a living miracle caused by a living God. It was my Lord Jesus Christ who protected him and delivered my brother from the hands of his captors. He deserves the honor and glory forever. The probability for people to survive a kidnapping in Mexico now is minimal. My brother did not have a chance to survive. He was mistakenly captured with the intention of killing him. That was the reason why we were not asked for ransom. When they found out that he was the wrong person it was too late. It was too risky for them to release him. He was in the hands of a powerful drug cartel. They charged him for all the expenses they incurred for his capture. He promised to keep his mouth shut to protect them as well as his own family. What had happened to my brother is very common in Mexico now. Headless bodies and corpses are found throughout the whole country. God was faithful to us and pulled out my brother alive from that dark hole where he was.

The prayers of my friends gave me faith and when faith exists miracles are bound to happen. Faith comes from the grace of our Lord Jesus Christ and it is given to us when we ask for. Many people prayed but not all the

40   Breaking Bondages

prayers were heard by God. The Bible says that God ignores our prayers when we are living in sin (Isaiah 59:2). Some prayers are responded by Satan who disguises himself as an angel of light (2Cor. 11:14). The idols cannot respond to the prayers because they are inanimate objects that cannot even remove their own dust. The Bible warns us against their worship in many of its books as we can see in this cite:

> They have mouths, but they do not speak;
> Eyes they have, but they do not see;
> They have ears, but they do not hear;
> Noses they have, but they do not smell;
> They have hands, but they do not handle;
> Feet they have, but they do not walk;
> Nor do they mutter through their throat.
> Those who make them are like them;
> So is everyone who trusts in them.
>
> Psalm 115:5-8

Jesus said that what we ask to the Father in His name will be granted (John 14:13). When we read the Scriptures we conclude that the devil deceived us, for there is only one God and only one mediator between God and us, the man Jesus Christ (1 Timothy 2:5).

The idolatry and ignorance of my family and friends is shameful. Every person that came to visit my brother said that they had promised to visit their saints in exchange for his freedom. No one said that they had made a promise to our Lord God. My eighty-year-old father, one of my brothers, and a nephew walked a distance of about 20 miles during the hottest time of the day to reward one of their idols. The whole family walked on their knees from the entrance of the temple to the altar of the Guadalupe virgin. A friend of the family came to ask us which sorcerer had helped us find him, so she could recommend it to others who were going through the same ordeal. Everything I saw and heard was outrageous. It is sad to hear that someone did something and all the credit is given to another person. How would you feel? I believe you would feel offended. That must be how our heavenly Father feels. How unfair we are due to our ignorance. All these happen because we do not read the Scriptures and learn the truth. These are the great offenses that bind us for generations to this world to do the will of the devil. God revealed to Paul that without Him we would be snarled, and instructs us to seek the release of humanity in the following scripture.

> *And a servant of the Lord must not quarrel but be gentle to all, able to teach, patient, in humility correcting those who are in opposition, if God perhaps will grant them repentance, so that they may know the truth, and that they may come to their senses and escape the snare of the devil, having been taken captive by him to do his will.*
>
> 2 Timothy 2:24-26

The Bible says that we are ensnared by the will of the devil. Satan is the king of the world and makes sure that we do not learn the truth. He placed Jesus on the top of a high mountain and showed Him in an instant all the kingdoms of the world. *"And the devil said to Him, 'All this authority I will give You, and their glory; for this has been delivered to me, and I give it to whomever I wish'"* (Luke 4:6). Who gave it to him? When God created Adam and Eve He told them to have dominion over everything created. They were the executive directors of His creation. But they ignored that they only had to follow God and also listened to the devil. They lost control of what was theirs and became a curse to the creation. The devil then became the king of the world. Since then, the devil has been deceiving mankind. He is making false miracles to keep people away from the truth which is God. The word of God describes people guided by the devil as follows, "unloving, unforgiving, slanderers, without self-control, brutal, despisers of good, traitors, headstrong, haughty, lovers of pleasure rather than lovers of God, having a form of godliness but denying its power. And from such people turn away!" (2 Timothy 3:3-5). I was just like that before meeting God. I wanted to have the best of everything not caring about the suffering of others, or God's will.

Chapter 5

Recovering the Lost Kingdom

Then God blessed them, and God said to them, "Be fruitful and multiply; fill the earth and subdue it; have dominion over the fish of the sea, over the birds of the air, and over every living thing that moves on the earth."

Genesis 1:28

The lordship of man was lost after the sin of the first man and woman. Adam and Eve were masters and lords of all the living things. They just had to obey one rule that God gave them. God instructed them not to eat from the tree of knowledge of good and evil. Upon the disobedience of Adam and Eve, God began to develop a plan of salvation to restore the lost kingdom. Although the Lord was very upset at man, He still decided to save them. He began to send messages of hope through his prophets and heralds. The coming of a Savior to the world was announced in the first book of the Bible. After the sin of the first man and woman every person was born with a depraved nature. The evil in the world was so bad that God regretted having made man (Genesis 6: 6).

God said He was going to destroy all the living creatures yet even in His anger, He had great compassion. The moment He saved Noah and his family from perishing, God was demonstrating that He did not want the human race to disappear. Eight persons survived the flood along with the animals. Unfortunately, the devil did not disappear and he is the one causing all the problems. The survivors were descendants from Adam and Eve; therefore, they were born imperfect and susceptible to fall in the traps of the devil.

The human race started to multiply and with them their evil desires. They were born prone to sin, so the devil began to tempt them where they were most vulnerable. After the sin, the Spirit of God separated from the human body. Communication between God and man was lost because the Spirit who was the link was not there. Without the helper or the Holy Spirit it is difficult to abstain from fleshly lusts. Humanity's corruption continued to the extent in which God could not stand it. His wrath was poured out once again. I'm talking about the judgment of Sodom and Gomorrah which were two cities destroyed by fire from above as punishment for both homosexuality and corruption. Again there were survivors and the human race continued existing. Parallel to the extent that humanity was growing, sin multiplied. God never gives up on us, no matter how much He suffers. He continued working on His salvation plan through which He had to sacrifice His own life. Grace was a tremendous need in the world due to the abundance of sin. In the appointed time, He sent His only son Jesus Christ to save us by paying a very high price for our freedom.

The Bible is a difficult book to read

Your word is a lamp to my feet, And a light to my path.
Psalm 119:105

It is very hard to convince people that the Bible is the sacred book provided for us by our Lord Jesus Christ. Salvation depends on the truth written in that book; therefore it is crucial to read it. If what we are taught

Recovering the Lost Kingdom   45

by our spiritual leaders is not in this book then it is heresy. It is true that ordinary men like us wrote the Bible. It is also true the Holy Spirit inspired these ordinary men. How do we know this? Jesus is God and He referred to the Pentateuch and other books while He was teaching in the world. The Pentateuch is comprised of the first five books of the Bible. He also cited the book of the prophets as if they were word of God. He did not mention the Koran or the book of Mormon or any other written document. There are many factors that prevent people from reading the Holy Scriptures. One of these factors is religions. They inculcate that the only thing we need to do to be saved is to follow their doctrines. Their leaders will speak to people in a very convincing tone to the point of making them lose their self-will. There are other people who think they know it all and are enclosed into their ignorance. Others believe that they do not need to look for the truth if they are not causing harm to anyone. Many believe that their works are going to save them. Behind all these factors are the artifices of the devil. The problem here is that there is no salvation if we choose to ignore the truth. Jesus is the path to follow in order to arrive to heaven. He is the way, the truth and the life; if we do not know Him, how do we expect to arrive to God? It is not enough to be good and not harm anyone just as it is not enough to follow one religion. We must believe in Jesus and follow His commandments.

Jesus told us to search the scriptures, not to have the Bible hidden or closed. Unless we read the Scriptures, we will continue walking in the dark pleasing the devil. He is the prince of the air and of every one that disobeys the Word of God. If we do not know the Word of God we are unarmed and exposed to be devoured by wolves dressed in sheep's clothing. Jesus said that those wolves would come in which we would defeat with the armor of light. "And take the helmet of salvation, and the sword of the Spirit, which is the word of God;" (Ephesians 6:17). God desires to have a relationship with us and the only thing He asks from us is obedience. He wants to bless us but we reject Him. He cannot come near us because of his immense purity. If He approaches us we will die and He wants to protect our lives. For this reason, He sent to us His Word through manuscripts. Those who do not have a relationship with God do not have a clue on how much the Creator suffers for us. We often suffer for the sake of our loved ones and our love does not compare to that of God. How much more must He suffer, He who is only love? When I imagine the Father's suffering I become anxious. I wish to run out into the world and tell everyone that He loves us all very much. God suffers way too much for our indifference. At the time when He was arrested and tortured His disciples were not there. Regardless of that, He proceeded with His plan for His love for us was above all suffering.

When I was a little girl the adults would say that those who read the Bible would go crazy. They shared stories of people losing their mind by reading the Bible. Obviously they did not know God to believe that He created the book with the intention of harming people. That statement is obviously an idea of Satan to keep people disarmed so he could do as he pleases. Others say that they do not read the Bible because they would have to change religions. I ask myself why people want a religion that hides the truth from them. Do you not wonder why some people are preventing us from reading the Bible? Or why do they tell us to read it in a certain way? Is it because they are hiding the truth? Is it that they fear losing something? To look for the truth is a matter of life or death. The truth is found in the Holy Scriptures and it will guide us to the salvation of our soul. The teachers are in the book as we read it in the following verse:

And though the Lord gives you
The bread of adversity and the water of affliction,
Yet your teachers will not be moved into a corner anymore,
But your eyes shall see your teachers.
Isaiah 30:20

Another verse states this: *Then you will know the truth, and the truth will set you free* (John 8:32). When we refuse to look for the truth we are rejecting Jesus who with so much love and pain gave his life for us. His sacrifice would be worthless because He died to save everybody, and not only for just a few. God could force us to seek the truth but He does not want anyone to come to Him except by his/her own will.

The Word of God is a light that God provided to enlighten the human race. Jesus throughout His Word guides our steps so that we will not stumble through the darkness in the world as indicated by the following passage. *"Then Jesus spoke to them again, saying, "I am the light of the world. He who follows Me shall not walk in darkness, but have the light of life"* (John 8:12 NRSV). We sometimes think that we know everything; however the biblical passage above says that without Jesus we are walking in the dark. While we are walking in the darkness, we are unable to defend ourselves. The devil takes hold of and destroys us with his claws. I perhaps should not speak about my brother's kidnapping by the delicacy of the matter but I am doing it to express my gratitude to God and to the people who had compassion for him. Also to tell those who have caused so much damage that we have forgiven them. We are praying that God would forgive them as well, guide their path and give them love so they would stop causing so much harm to others and be saved. I said love because that is what the world is lacking. It is the greatest gift God has given us. *"For God so loved the world that He gave His only begotten Son, that whoever believes in Him should not perish but have everlasting life"* (John 3:16). Paul said that love takes us to perfection which obviously is our Heavenly Father. When you behave in the way our Lord wants, you are serving other people with light, which in turn will make them happy, and will want to imitate us. "Most assuredly, I say to you, he who believes in Me, the works that I do he will do also; and greater *works* than these he will do, because I go to My Father" (John 14:12). God wants the world to shine with His light which is His own written Word.

Chapter 6

God Heals All Illness

And He came down with them and stood on a level place with a crowd of His disciples and a great multitude of people from all Judea and Jerusalem, and from the seacoast of Tyre and Sidon, who came to hear Him and be healed of their diseases, as well as those who were tormented with unclean spirits. And they were healed. And the whole multitude sought to touch Him, for power went out from Him and healed them all.

Luke 6:17-19

The miracles started to happen from the beginning of my walk with God. We had a weekly Bible study at home formed by mostly religious people. Regardless of our spiritual maturity we could see at least two miracles of healing in that setting. One occurred the first time we met. A woman from the same congregation was sick with pneumonia for several weeks. The doctor diagnosed her with cancer in the bronchioles. According to her doctors she had a tumor of the size of a tangerine and was in stage four. She was experiencing difficulty in speaking but still attended our first reunion. That day I asked God to prepare me with a special message for the reunion. Only 6 people came to the first meeting. Together we read a testimony narrated in a book. One person was healed by God from terminal cancer. After reading the testimony, together we prayed God to remove the tumor from that lady. My spiritual level was like that of a child. Kids believe everything, and as such I had faith that a miracle would occur. Indeed, two weeks later the doctors could not find the tumor. She was healed by our Lord Jesus Christ.

Another person was healed of cancer at my home. With the same group, we prayed for a twenty year old girl who had been diagnosed with cervical cancer for the second time. She was very nervous and did not know what to do. The girl was a friend of my daughter. My daughter invited her so we could pray for a miracle to happen in her life. The girl did not have any other options, so she accepted the invitation. She was not a Christian, and God was just an idea to her. The whole group prayed for her. We formed a circle around her and we declared her clean of any sickness in the name of our Lord Jesus Christ. Soon after that a miracle was confirmed. On her next visit to the doctor, she was told that the cancer had disappeared. Glory be to the Lord forever! They received the miracle and left happily. They never returned to the group. My desire is for them to at least take the time to thank God for such a great prodigy. In the Bible we read that worse things can happen to us if we do not change our old ways (John 5:14).

This other testimony was experienced within my family. Two great prodigies happened in one story. My sister's husband was suffering a terminal cancer that had invaded his entire body. It was believed that he was at the verge of death. He would not eat or speak anymore. His youngest son went to Mexico to see him for the last time. God gave him the opportunity to go on this trip by easing the immigration process that granted him a permit. He was able to go and return to the country to be able to reunite with his family. At this moment it is very difficult for Mexicans to obtain a permission to remain in this country. It seemed nearly impossible for my nephew since he had had problems with the law. In less than four months his application was approved without having to leave the country as it is required for almost all the applications. He was granted legal residency without asking him about

God Heals All Illness 51

his criminal record. God represented him in the interviews and the case was solved miraculously. During his one-week visit he was able to pray for the health of his father's body and soul. His recovery started to become noticeable soon after my nephew's prayers. Within a few weeks my brother-in-law began to regain energy and started to walk. He lived for two more years in which God gave him the opportunity to hear His Word and perhaps get right with Him. I claim the promise made for those who love and obey God's commandments. *"For the promise is to you and to your children, and to all who are afar off, as many as the Lord our God will call"* (Acts 2:39).

God never comes too late. Recently I met a middle-aged woman with a very sweet nature. We met through a divine appointment. I woke up with an urge to call a friend who was very pleased to hear from me. She asked me to come to her house to pray for her mom and there I met this lady. My friend's mother was a ninety-year-old lady who was very surprised to see me next to her. She did not know me but said that she saw me in her dream the night before. God was confirming that I was not there by accident. She proceeded to narrate her weird dream as soon as she saw me. The Lady that God sent over to my friend's house was suffering a nervous breakdown due to a heavy demonic oppression against her. She desperately needed prayers and the Lord sent me to pray for her, so that she would give me this testimony. Eighteen years ago this sister in Christ was diagnosed with an incurable cancer in the uterus. The doctor gave her 6 months to live. She decided to travel to El Salvador to spend her last days with her three little children. She also would prefer to die in her homeland with her loved ones. She hid her condition from her family in order to not sadden them. Quietly in her room she suffered the terrible pain caused by the cancer. The cancer of the uterus was causing her continuous bleeding which kept her enclosed in her room so that no one would notice. She would sleep in a hammock because of the bleeding since she had no strength to continue washing her bed sheets. In her bedroom she would pray to God to have mercy. She wanted to be healed to care for her small children.

One night, when her days seemed to be numbered, she cried out to God with all her heart. She cried and begged for her life until her strength faded and fell asleep. Soon after that a voice woke her up and told her to turn on the radio. As she turned it on, a woman said that this prayer time was dedicated for cancer liberation. She immediately realized she had to join in prayer with the radio. She placed her hand on the electronic device to pray with them. After the prayer she fell asleep and forgot about the incident. In the morning when she woke up, she noticed that her hemorrhage had ceased. She pressed her stomach and noticed that she no longer had pain where before could not even bear to touch. She got up full of energy and shared with her family the great prodigy. They all thanked God together for such a great miracle He had done for them. Her mother admitted to her that she knew what was happening. She finally communicated to her family that she had returned from the United States to die near them, but did not want to see them suffering. God performs these miracles to increase our faith. We cannot keep them to ourselves.

God cures addictions

Idolatry destroys us. A nephew of mine was terribly driven by the love of money. At the age of 16 he had already been selling drugs trying to impress the world with his dirty money. He started to earn a lot of money and his ambition for more increased greatly. He was blinded by the love of money and the popularity of those who have it. Soon after, he was arrested for possession of drugs and was incarcerated for one year. In jail he was invited to a Bible study which he attended just to do something. To him the Bible was like any other book but a specific phrase in the book of Revelation caught his attention. "He who has wisdom will understand what he reads." That night before he went to sleep he closed his eyes and asked God to give him wisdom. He wanted to understand what he read. After that he forgot all about it.

Right after he was released, he continued doing his dirty business. As the scriptures say, he was still tied to the world to do the devil's will. He thought he could serve the devil without being affected by him. He became a father at an early age due to his immaturity and lack of advice. A relationship between two immature people did not function. The ending of his relationship with his significant other left him hurt which took him to find intense refuge in alcohol. The tentacles of the devil began to imprison him. He soon found himself attracted to different addictions including gambling where he was losing all the money he earned. He met another girl who claimed to be a Christian but she did not practice the faith she professed. A few days after they had met each other, they moved in together without being married. Very soon she decided to leave him as she did not see any future with their relationship. He got depressed and began to use drugs and to drink more alcohol trying to dispel his sorrows. Not being able to find the relief in the substances he was consuming he attempted to take his own life. He put a rope around his neck and hanged himself to try to put an end to all his sufferings. When he noticed that he was no longer feeling oxygen he changed his mind. With great effort, he was able to untie himself from the rope that was choking him. He continued living because God had another plan in his life although he was not free of his addictions yet. He was losing all his dignity. His ex-girlfriend found him and returned with him but he was already an addict to drugs and alcohol. He was fired from his job for he was being accused of stealing from the company.

The love of money is at the root of all evil (1 Tim. 6:10). My nephew continued living a life of fantasy where money means everything. For him God was just a made up story fashioned to keep us in fear. But although he did not believe in God, God believed in him. One day something extraordinary happened in his life. To be precise, it was on July 7th, 2007 when a soft voice spoke to him telling him to not be afraid of anything because He was his shield. He tried ignoring the voice but he just could not. That same night he was instructed by God to look for a Bible. At midnight he went to Walmart to buy one that he immediately began to read. The Lord opened his eyes and he was able to see what God had done for us. The Holy Spirit convinced him of all the harm he was causing to humanity as well as to himself. Driven by the desire to follow the one who gave his life for us, he took the forty pounds of marijuana in his possession and threw it away in a river nearby. He flushed into the toilet all of the cocaine and alcohol he had. This is something that should not be done because of the damage it could cause marine life. He just wanted to get rid of those evils as quickly as possible. With anger he uprooted a marijuana plant in his back yard as a symbol of his desire to remove the root of all evil that existed in him. From that moment Christ liberated him from all of his addictions.

Who God frees, is free indeed. He did not need to attend any rehab group or ask for any kind of psychological help. He trusted in God, which through His word was assuring him that he would be free. "Then you will know the truth, and the truth will set you free." (John 8:32) That day Jesus, the son of God, set him free and never again returned to doing drugs. He was baptized with the fire of the Holy Spirit as spoken by John the Baptist. "I indeed baptize you with water unto repentance, but He who is coming after me is mightier than I, whose sandals I am not worthy to carry. He will baptize you with the Holy Spirit and fire" (Matthew 3:11). Now his greatest desire is to win souls for Christ. He now serves as an associate pastor at a Christian church and hopes soon to travel the world preaching the good news of salvation. He wanted to share his testimony with the desire to bring hope to those who at this moment are living bound to the world of alcohol and drugs. If Christ rescued him, He would rescue you too if you believe it.

Chapter 7

Persistence with Faith Moves God

Then He spoke a parable to them, that men always ought to pray and not lose heart, saying: "There was in a certain city a judge who did not fear God nor regard man. Now there was a widow in that city; and she came to him, saying, 'Get justice for me from my adversary.' And he would not for a while; but afterward he said within himself, 'Though I do not fear God nor regard man, yet because this widow troubles me I will avenge her, lest by her continual coming she weary me."

Luke 18:1-5

God responds to our requests when we express them with faith. During the time of my family's tragedies I had two jobs as a teacher and was also finishing my Masters in School Administration. It is difficult to do all of these things for anyone, especially when besides that you have four children to care for. Imagine how it was for me to pretend to be normal when the world around me was spinning rapidly. The exam to obtain my Master's degree was offered to me two weeks after my mother's death. I had only one chance to pass this exam. There was so much going on in my head I was not able to concentrate on one thing. God was my only solution. Every night before going to bed I would tell Him that I wanted to pass that exam and I was depending on Him solely. Meanwhile the devil was pushing hard to make sure that I failed it.

I received my admission ticket to the exam with the wrong time. The night before my exam I supplicated one more time to God to have mercy on me. After praying for a while I randomly opened the Bible seeking for God's wisdom. As soon as I opened it, I perceived a strange feeling. There was a very comforting message. The Lord spoke to me through the parable of the man knocking at odd hours of the night at the friend's house asking for bread. The friend denies the assistance arguing that it's very late. He refuses to get up to give him what he is asking because his children are asleep. The man knocking does not give up and insisted many times. Finally the friend gets up and gives him what he is asking. He does not give it to him because he is his friend but because of his insistency (Luke 11:7). It was very clear to me that my heavenly Father had listened to my pleas. Also a thought came to my mind as if someone had spoken to me loud and clear. "You are the same person to me with or without that degree, but I will help you because of your insistence and perseverance. He was telling me I did not need a degree to please or serve Him. My admissions ticket stated that my exam would begin at 9:00 in the morning but the real time scheduled was at 8:00 a.m. That morning I received a call from a friend informing me that my ticket had an error. She advised me to leave immediately. I left on time and I was able to take the exam thanks to my heavenly Father. The Holy Spirit guided me and gave me the adequate answers to pass the exam. Honor and glory are to my God forever.

God Calms the Storm

Our lives are threatened by different types of storms. I am speaking both

Persistence with Faith Moves God   57

literally and figuratively. The Bible describes a storm which was unleashed while Jesus was in a boat with the fishermen. The fishermen grew scared while Jesus tranquilly slept rocked by the waves. When they were in the border of despair they woke Him up. Jesus, confided in his power, ordered for the storm to halt and it stopped. The next testimony I am sharing was short but intense. I found myself being very nervous because of an interview I was going to attend in order to receive my Pastorate license. When I arrived at the place I saw a room full of judges. My nerves betrayed me and I began to shake. The interview was not in my native language and this made me feel insecure. In desperation I cried out to God who comforted me using a Bible passage:

Now it happened, on a certain day, that He got into a boat with His disciples.
And He said to them, "Let us cross over to the other side of the lake."
And they launched out. But as they sailed He fell asleep.
And a windstorm came down on the lake, and they were filling with water,
and were in jeopardy. And they came to Him and
woke Him, saying, "Master, Master, we are perishing!"
Then He arose and rebuked the wind and the raging of the water.
And they ceased, and there was a calm.
But He said to them, "Where is your faith?"
And they were afraid, and marveled, saying to one another,
"Who can this be? For He commands even the winds
and water, and they obey Him!
Luke 8:22-25

As soon as I read the passage I told my heavenly Father I was leaving the situation in His hands. He quickly responded and came to calm the storm. Five minutes later I was being interviewed and my responses seemed to be surprising the interviewers. They would make positive comments emphasizing the little time I had known God personally, which was only 3 years. After my interview I was asked to step out so they could discuss my answers. In less than five minutes and before I knew it I was called in again to be told that everyone had approved me unanimously. Then and there I

58 Breaking Bondages

was invited to share my testimonies to a congregation and preach in another.

God calms the storms. This other testimony was compared with the movie "The Perfect Storm" by the way it was handled. This was a test to my patience and self-control. One day when I was working as Dean of students, the worst students from the entire school were sent to my office. There were more than a dozen students sent there to avoid classroom interruptions. It was a testing week to measure the school's academic achievement. The teachers could not handle the students so they were sent to an opportunity room to take the test. When they finished testing, all of them were sent to my office. I was told that they carelessly and quickly answered and turned in the test. A woman who was volunteering in the dean's office contradicted my orders to the students in front of them. I asked her to allow me to do my job but she ignored me. As a penalty for their rebellion in class, the students had to solve some math problems. She told them that they did not have to do anything since they were done with their exam. I nicely asked the lady to leave the office. Before leaving she insulted me expressing an angry feeling about the way I performed my job. Then she went to the administration to complain about me to the principal. The students took advantage of the situation to disrespect me by laughing and teasing me. They were so insolent that I had to call security. The security guards arrived but when they saw the chaos going on decided to leave. They knew that it would be very difficult to control that situation. The administrators came and everyone left the office frustrated because the students ignored them too. The office sounded like a kennel as to the noise but even worse when it came to what the students were saying.

I prayed to God for help and He did not leave me alone. I stood by the door praying silently while God gave me peace and self-control. It was clear to me that controlling the situation was beyond human effort. Every time I was left alone in the office, the students stopped their insolence. When someone came to try to control them, the students went crazy. The jokes they would make about me were very cruel. It was very hard not to lose control but God was with me. The students would become upset knowing that their insults and mockery did not affect me. Everyone was surprised to see the self-control in me. If it was not for God, I would have ran away or who knows what else. The school administrators called the police and a few patrols came to arrest the students. The ones who were not arrested were suspended for days. When they arrived at the office, they were surprised to see me alone with them. What surprised them the most was to see that I was calm. The principal ignored the lady who started the problem, so she went to the central offices to complain about me. No one listened to her lies and everything ended peacefully. Glory be to God.

God's Help Knows No Limits

God is always there for us if we seek Him with our heart. It does not matter what we need, we can always depend on God. This example I am narrating sounds silly but it shows divine intervention. My sons took blankets to an abandoned house and brought bedbugs into my house. The parasites quickly and silently took over the whole house without us noticing. When we found out what was causing us all of our skin bites we started to look for solutions. We bought many products trying to combat the plague. We would wash all of the bed covers and blankets weekly but nothing seemed to work. It was exhausting and depressing because all our efforts were in vain. In desperation, I called God for help. I remembered that the Bible recommends us to cast our cares and burdens to our heavenly Father that He would alleviate our worries (1 Peter 5:6-7). I told God I was going to leave Him this load of mine and that I confided in his Word. Then I asked my husband if we could go to the beach to spend the weekend there. We wanted a break away from the bugs.

The answer to my prayers came immediately. My youngest daughter wanted a hotel with a pool, but we could not find one near the beach in that city. We looked around and we finally found one in the center of the city away from the beach. It was dark when we went to swim. There were four people inside the pool: a couple and two teenagers. The adults were in the Jacuzzi. We got into the Jacuzzi and started a conversation with the couple. While we were in the Jacuzzi, the man's cell phone rang and he got out to answer it. He returned a bit annoyed saying that he had to work the next day which was Sunday. I was curious and asked him what kind of job he had. The moment I heard his answer I knew God had sent him to help us. He was a bedbug exterminator, and worked there at the hotel because they too had the plague there. We hired him there after negotiating a very reasonable price compared to other exterminator companies. The low price made my husband doubt about the effectiveness of the job. I asked him to trust in God and he did it. The exterminator promised to exterminate the bugs in three treatments. He drove over one hour (without traffic) to get to my house every week.

We were supposed to help each other but I did not know that. The first day he came to our house we received him happily because our problem was going to be solved. I tried to witness to him about God because that is what fills my heart but he politely avoided me. He informed me that he was very religious and knew everything about God. He asked me to step out of the house to start his job. Eight hours later we returned home and did not find the cats we had left in the garage. It was strange because our cats always refuse to put a foot outside of the house. My daughters looked for them throughout the whole neighborhood and did not find them. We were sure they had been devoured by the coyotes and animals around the hills in our town. My daughters were very upset, blaming me for not closing the back door of the garage, which leads to the patio. While my daughters looked for the cats, inside the house my two sons were fighting violently for no apparent reason. The situation in my house became chaotic and out of control. When I saw that things were getting worse I went to my room to pray for help. The Lord quickly came to my rescue and told me what to do. The Holy Spirit led me to anoint the whole house with olive oil. I followed the advice and started to rebuke the evil spirits who had taken away the peace of my home. Minutes after the anointing, the cats returned home and everything went back to normal. The exterminator returned three more times to fumigate the house. Every time he came I tried to witness to him about God but he always refused to listen. He promised to return one more time to make sure that the plague was exterminated, but there was not a fifth time.

The weekend came but the exterminator did not return to collect his money. My husband and I called him many times but no one would answer. Three weeks later his ex-wife called my husband, since there were many missed calls from his number. She asked if her ex-husband owed us money. She informed my husband that Jose, her ex-husband, had committed suicide. The news affected me very much. I blamed myself for not witnessing effectively to one God had assigned to me. God had put Jose in my path because He knew his heart and did not want him to be a lost one. I had to preach the gospel to him so he would be saved to avoid this sad ending. God did not fail in helping me get rid of the bedbugs but I probably could have done something better. I could have been more persistent but I was weak and I failed. This situation taught me a great lesson. It also gave me the discernment to get to know the influence of the spirits in our lives. Jose was surrounded by a strong spirit of death. The evil spirits invaded my house. They were so strong that they scared my two cats to leave home for more than eight hours. They also caused my children to hit each other with whatever was in front of them. Those spirits did not enter my house after the anointing but they took Jose to the grave ignoring God's love. He categorically rejected the person sent by God to witness to him the truth and bring peace to his life.

God protects us in every situation

My job as a Dean of students sixth through twelve grade is a tough one. The rebel students disrespect and humiliate adults. Trying to discipline students leads us to their families where the problems usually began. One morning the school principal called me up to her office to inform me about something but she forgot. When I arrived at her office she was speaking to a twelfth grade girl. She invited me to listen to their conversation. During the conversation the principal mentioned three times about the same biblical verse: "No weapon formed against you shall prosper, And every tongue *which* rises against you in judgment You shall condemn" (Isaiah 54:17a). The principal wanted to tell me that students planned to have a food fight where both she and I would be the target of their attacks. When I found out about the food fight I was confident. I walked through the tables praying and singing quietly praises to God. The cafeteria was full with hundreds of students. I saw when they began to throw the first thing and approached the student to scold him. As I approached the boy, I heard a whistle that called them to action. They all responded at once by throwing all the food to one another and to anyone passing by. It took them about two minutes to completely throw everything and empty the cafeteria running off. I stood in the middle of the cafeteria shocked and surprised that they did not hit me with any food. I saw other adults who supervised the area soaked with milk, juices, sauces, etc., while I was clean. I was in the middle of the fight and was not touched. Then I remembered God had warned me of the danger. He also assured me He would protect me if they had tried to hit me. I thanked my heavenly Father for His promises that say He will never forsake us (Psalm 42:8). That incident increased my faith. It gave me the confidence to face anything knowing that the angel of the Lord encamps around those who fear Him (Psalm 34:7).

Chapter 8

God Always Answers to our Prayers

If you abide in Me, and My words abide in you,
you will ask what you desire, and it shall be done for you.

John 15: 7

We must pray according to God's will. I moved to work in another school but I kept driving the same way for a year. My son wanted to finish high school in that school and I had to take him to the subway every day. One day while driving, a banner shaped like a hand caught my attention. It was a psychic announcing her divination and quackery services in a residential area. At that moment I remembered the Word of God states He hates those things. The zeal of God filled me and at that instant I made a declaration. I proclaimed in the name of Jesus of Nazareth that the sign would disappear from there. Every day when I passed by that house I would declare by faith the posting would be removed. I declared this for almost one year. With only one week before my son's graduation the sign remained. I would not have to pass by anymore and that concerned me for a moment but I prayed again. During the next weekend something incredible happened. With great joy I beheld what God made. Not only the hand with the sign was gone but the whole house was completely demolished. It was obvious that the person who bought that place did not agree with the pagan practices of their former owners. Today, instead of that ad there is a green palm tree that represents the soul of the righteous. That deed was a great testimony not only for me but also for my child who saw me praying every day I passed by. We learned that our prayers have power when they are presented with faith in agreement with God's will.

One day I went to the mountain seeking the presence of God. I wanted to be alone with the Creator for I felt a void in my heart. I was not getting the spiritual nourishment I needed. I reached the top of a hill near my house and I started talking to God. I wanted him to speak to me as He did with Moses, Elijah and other people from the Scriptures. I wanted to have a supernatural experience although I do not deserve it. I prayed for a while then I waited to hear God's voice but nothing happened. I sadly started my way down the hill with the same hunger for God. I was at the bottom of the mountain when God whispered something to me. He instructed me to fast to be prepared for something He would do. I returned home determined to start a fast that would strengthen my spirit. I fasted for twenty-one days led by God. Seven days were without eating anything, just drinking fluids. The other fourteen days I only ate fruits and vegetables. During those days I felt very close to God. He was leading me in prayer. I asked for drastic changes in my life. In the first week He sent me to speak with the leaders of the church where I was an associate pastor. The message was we should leave our comfort zone to glorify God in all that we did. I suggested that we should join in fasting and prayer seeking God's direction for the new year just beginning. The message was not well received and in three days I was fired by the pastor. He said I could not serve as leader of that church because I was spiritually immature. He feared to lose other members of the congregation if he changed things.

God immediately provided another place to study His Word. Since I was released, I had to find another place to meet with the group I was leading.

The Spanish group followed me although they knew that I did not have a place to meet. We met at my house to pray and the Lord led us to fast. We asked God where we should meet. Three days later, early in the morning the Lord whispered to me that we could meet at the school where I work. I was surprised at the answer but I believed Him. When I arrived at the school instead of going to my office, I went to the principal's office. I asked her to lend me the auditorium and I got it without any objection. Now we meet there weekly, and do not have to depend on anyone or pay any rent. The Lord brought these drastic changes I asked for. He sent us workers for this new job and the church is growing for the honor and glory of God.

Chapter 9

God Continues to Send Disciples to Baptize People

But you shall receive power when the Holy Spirit has come upon you; and you shall be witnesses to Me in Jerusalem, and in all Judea and Samaria, and to the end of the earth.

Acts 1:8

Jesus left a commission two thousand years ago and it is still effective now. When we surrender our lives completely to God, He leads and uses us according to His plan of salvation. First He molds and equips us so we can be useful for the mission. One morning I woke up with an intense desire to immediately travel to Mexico. The trip was already planned by my heavenly Father. The trip had divine appointments for each of the twelve days there. When my husband asked me how many days I would stay in Mexico, without hesitating, I answered twelve. God also sent my nephew on this trip as He did with the apostles and the 72 disciples, who were sent two by two. Satan tried to stop this trip by damaging the airplanes, that way we

68   Breaking Bondages

would not reach our destination but he failed. It was not a coincidence that we both had our flights delayed for many hours. These setbacks were used to evangelize at the airport. They even allowed me to visit the sick in hospitals where several people received Christ. God uses everything to accomplish His plans: *"And we know that all things work together for good to those who love God, to those who are the called according to His purpose"* (Romans 8:28). We thought we were going there to evangelize my brother, but it was not for him. He was just the hook that pulled us over there to liberate others.

After I learned the plane my nephew travelled on was delayed I received a call from a friend. She was asking me to visit her sick cousin in a hospital in Guadalajara. Ironically, several weeks ago she had expressed her desire that someone could take the gospel to her cousin that she feared would die soon. I never thought it would be me. The delay of my nephew's plane forced me to stay in Guadalajara waiting for him. It also allowed me the chance to witness to a few people in a hospital as well as in the airport. It was an adventure trying to find the hospital as if someone was trying very hard to stop me. I did my best and finally got to see her. All the people who I asked where the hospital was gave me wrong directions that led me to other hospitals. When I finally reached the civil hospital, the time was pressing. I had to be back at the airport in just over an hour. In less than an hour of preaching there, I saw three people in the hospital room inviting Christ into their hearts including my friend's cousin. Glory be to God!

The rain was our ally to win people for Christ. The trip from Guadalajara to Zamora is normally done in two hours. The heavy rain slowed us down and it took over four hours to arrive at our destination. The rain served to give us more time to take the message of salvation to my family. Two days later my sister wanted to be baptized to show obedience to God and thus receive the gift of the Holy Spirit. In another village the creek's water shrank so my niece could be baptized in its waters. Two days earlier we visited that stream which invited us back to enjoy its waters. When we returned the stream was not attractive to the people who were with us. The whole family who was joining us changed their plans on swimming in that river and instead went to the ocean. My niece and I decided to stay at the creek where I witnessed to her. I shared with her the story of the eunuch and Philip and right after that she asked to be baptized there. There was a pond that allowed the christening to take place. If the family had been present with all their skepticism and religiosity, the baptism would not have been possible.

God prepared divine appointments for each day of our trip. We went from place to place preaching the gospel and baptizing people in the name of the Father, the Son and the Holy Spirit. During the twelve days the trip lasted many people received the gospel and five were baptized. Those baptized are the pioneers to bring the truth to the people in the villages we visited. The Spirit of God will equip them for the great work of evangelization. Every time we witnessed to people, we shared what Peter recommended to the Jews. *"Then Peter said to them, 'Repent, and let every one of you be baptized in the name of Jesus Christ for the remission of sins; and you shall receive the gift of the Holy Spirit'"* (Acts 2:38).

Fasting is a good discipline when we are seeking for God's direction. In my prayers, I asked God to give me the opportunity to serve him. My prayer partners and I decided to do a corporate fast for seven days trying to be more sensitive to God's voice. At the end of the week the Lord opened a door. We were invited to visit convalescent hospitals. The first day we visited one of them, I was asked to share a few words with patients. Unprepared I stood in front of that congregation and clearly felt like the Lord put words in my mouth. The message of salvation was followed by the invitation to receive the Lord. The Word of God spoke to them and soon after a few people opened their heart to Christ. Now every time I visit those places I delight to see how many people are asking Jesus to be their Lord and Savior. The Word of God says that the fields are white; the crops are ready and we can see evidence of that at the hospitals. Every day patients receive Christ and are baptized right there following the examples of the early church described in the Book of Acts. Then we laid hands on praying to God to give them the gift of the Spirit as He has promised (Acts 2:38).

God reveals his plans to us

God leads us to walk in the right path. When I was looking for a church where I could learn more about God, the Lord sent me to a Christian church. It was very hard to attend a church that was not Catholic. Every time I visited a Christian church I returned home upset for no reason. One day after I returned from a church I went to my room to speak to God about my distress related with the Christian churches. That day I clearly sensed or heard when God asked me that if I wanted to know Him or if wanted to continue in my religion. I responded that I wanted to get closer to him but I did not know how. He led me to repudiate the spirit of Catholicism and that day I was freed to follow God. That same week the Lord showed me a church, but the devil tried to discourage me. When my husband suggested that we attended it, I objected to it because it was far away from everything. The first time we visited it I felt something very special there. I was crying but this time it was because the presence of God was very strong near me. For nearly three years I attended that congregation where I learned to read the scriptures and talk to God. God baptized me with the Holy Spirit and with much fire.

The fire of the Holy Spirit ignited me to grow spiritually faster than others. The day came when I was no longer spiritually satisfying for me in that congregation. The Lord led me in prayer early in the morning seeking direction. One day early in the morning, the Lord led me to pray for revival in the church. I prayed for revival several weeks and then I sent an email to the pastor. I explained how God had guided me to pray for that congregation. The Lord was promising to bring a spiritual awakening to the church if we worshipped Him more in that sanctuary. He wanted the congregation to freely worship in spirit and in truth with songs and dances. The pastor recommended that I submit the idea to the church board. The board decided that it was not the right time for changes in the program. They had more important things to do in those days. Their priorities were more important than those of God.

The Lord confirmed that what I had said came from Him. A few weeks after presenting the idea of more worship, we had an amazing manifestation of His glory in the sanctuary. It happened on a Sunday when almost all the men of the congregation went to a retreat for a weekend. While I was praying at church before Sunday service, I sensed that God was telling me that He was going to be near us. The Lord revealed to me that He would manifest in that sanctuary as they had never felt Him before. I asked God

God Continues to Send Disciples to Baptize People   71

for confirmation on the message received. I suggested that someone from the prayer group would hold my hand. I walked to the other side of the room I stayed there praying. While I was there a girl came over to me, took me by the hand and together we prayed for revival.

The Lord is amazing. When the prayer session was over we went to the sanctuary to hear the sermon of that day. I was very surprised to find out that there was no pastor that day in the church. The worship team was leading the congregation in prayer and worshipping. I got on my knees and began to pray while the group sang praises. They played instruments and praised God with hymns and songs. I was convinced to remain on my knees until the Lord fulfilled His promise. I was getting anxious but I did not move up. The worship leader sat at the piano to play the last song. When we were half way through the last song, the worship leader began to mourn and could not continue singing. She stood up very excited and began to ask the congregation to share their testimonies. People stood up from every side of the sanctuary sharing testimonies and crying. Some people publicly confessed sins that had never dared to confess to anyone. The youth cried and wondered if that was a revival. The presence of God was so strong that all eyes were wet that day in the sanctuary. When the euphoria had happened the service was concluded. People did not want to leave because they wanted to talk about what happened. They looked at each other surprised and excited. I got up from the floor and walked towards the partner who took my hands in the prayer room. She was on the other side of the sanctuary. As I approached her to share about our exciting experience, an enormous strength shook me while a fear gripped me. I hugged her trying to hide behind her body because I felt so unworthy and dirty. The purity of God exposes our faults and mine were revealed that day.

The Lord showed the congregation His desire for more worshipping in that sanctuary. He was telling us that we should worship Him more instead of following traditions. God also was showing the leaders that this was not my idea but His. Next time I saw the pastor I reminded him about extending the service of worship and praise. I explained that God had confirmed my words the day when he was not there. I challenged him to ask the congregation who was present the day of revival including his wife. He responded that it was not my job to tell him what to do. He arrogantly said that God communicated with him as well. From that day on the pastor avoided me. During those days, many members of the congregation began to move to other congregations. The tension in that place was strong. My husband and I started to talk about moving to another church. We did not know where to go. I began to pray for direction again. I asked God to tell us to choose from two possible prospects. The Lord sent me to another church of the same denomination through a dream. In the dream God dismissed me from the former church and freed me to go to another. When my husband and daughters saw that I was serious about moving churches they backed down and kept going to the same one we had attended. I asked the Lord to release them too if He was moving me. God is always wise and soon did what I asked him. I sent a letter to the former pastor thanking him for everything I learned in that church and explained that God had moved me to another. This email unlike others previously sent was answered quickly. In it he offended me very much. He was talking about my mistakes and my faults, which I told him in confidence. I was unfairly blamed for many things. He also gave a bad recommendation to my new pastor. This letter served to free my husband and my daughters from that church. Once again God was showing that He works in everything for the good of those who love him. Regardless of the bad recommendation, a month later I was appointed Associate Pastor in charge of the Spanish ministry by the board of my new church. Glory be to God!

Chapter 10

The False Teachers

But there were also false prophets among the people, even as there will be false teachers among you, who will secretly bring in destructive heresies, even denying the Lord who bought them, and bring on themselves swift destruction. And many will follow their destructive ways, because of whom the way of truth will be blasphemed. By covetousness they will exploit you with deceptive words; for a long time their judgment has not been idle, and their destruction does not slumber.

2 Peter 2:1-3

The apostasy is in its maximum expression lately. False prophets and teachers are a danger to the church today. The Holy Scriptures warn us about false teachers and prophets. These false teachers usually know the truth, but deliberately lie because it suits their interests. Their pursuits include money, fame, selfishness and the desire to please people. They do not teach the truth for they fear that people would not come back. The quality of the church is measured by the number of people attending on a weekly basis. If the number surpasses the two hundreds they are known as healthy churches. They plan activities to entertain the families and keep them comfortable to make sure they become active members of their congregations. Their outreach ways are made through music concerts, drama plays and famous speakers who are wolves in disguise. Today most churches teach what people want to hear as the Scriptures say: "For the time will come when they will not endure sound doctrine, but according to their own desires, *because* they have itching ears, they will heap up for themselves teachers; and they will turn *their* ears away from the truth, and be turned aside to fables" (2 Timothy 4:3-4).

The leaven of the Pharisees in these times has been mixed with the bread of life which is the Word of God. The spiritual food people now receive from the wolves in disguise is shifting their five senses. Wrong is seen as right and dirty is considered as clean based on the new standards of the current church. The pastors and evangelists are trading and profiting from the things of God. They create a god in their own image based on their man-made doctrines and precepts. There are hundreds of false doctrines that make people believe that going to church every week and tithing is all they need to be saved. Jesus warns us about the wolves dressed in sheep's skin. They are very good actors which with empty words deceive people that entrust their children which end up being raped. They are always asking for money to expand the kingdom of God but in reality what they are expanding is the kingdom of darkness.

> *But know this, that in the last days perilous times will come: For men will be lovers of themselves, lovers of money, boasters, proud, blasphemers, disobedient to parents, unthankful, unholy, unloving, unforgiving, slanderers, without self-control, brutal, despisers of good, traitors, headstrong, haughty, lovers of pleasure rather than lovers of God, having a form of godliness but denying its power. And from such people turn away!*
> 2 Timothy 3:1-5

We are currently living in the last days as referred in the above passage.

The False Teachers   75

The sad thing is that the passage very well describes our spiritual leaders. We must be very alert to not be confused by those men who pretend to be godly. Our creed must be based on the Word of God and have as teacher the Holy Spirit guiding us to understand it. What I am saying here is that we should pray to God to give us teachers full of the Holy Spirit. In today's world it is very common to hear people saying that the Lord told them to say or do things and the Lord never said that. All the past and future prophecies are written in the Holy Scriptures. God finished all his work on the sixth day. If they are not in there, they are not from God because the Bible is the only book fully inspired by God. What I mean by this is that the apparitions of virgins and other images that people worship are not from God. Both the Old and New Testaments warn us not to have other gods or any image to worship. It is the first of the Ten Commandments given to the Israelites through Moses (Exodus 20:4).

Idolatry is practiced everywhere. Who do you think is behind all idolatry and deceit? It is obviously the devil because there is only good and evil nothing between. Yes, the devil is delivering his last blows in a hurry because clearly he knows his time is running out. That is why at this time there is a fever of false miracles and apparitions even in tortillas. But I am not surprised! The Bible states that Satan disguises himself as an angel of light (2 Corinthians 11:14). The devil does not want us to read the Bible so that we continue to ignore the truth, but he reads it well. The devil knows by heart the Word of God otherwise he would not act the way he does. He uses it to manipulate the world through the use of corrupt leaders. If you do not believe me that it is crucial for us to read the Bible, at least imitate the devil and read it out of curiosity. The truth is based solely on the Word of God and is revealed to us by His Holy Spirit. Anyone who proclaims Christ as Lord and Savior and lives in obedience to His Word is true. There are hundreds of religions and false doctrines but the Bible speaks of two particularly. The one that forbids people to get married and the one that prohibits eating certain foods. The Bible calls them doctrines of the devil. These people are hypocrites and liars, and their consciences are dead. God instructs His servants to be married to avoid conflicts at church. About the food He says that we should not call anything dirty. We can eat anything thanking the Lord for the provision (1

76   Breaking Bondages

Timothy 4:2-3). Let's make sure that we do not take part with them.

We have two revelations of God for our spiritual growth. One revelation is physical and that is our Lord Jesus Christ. *"And the Word became flesh and dwelt among us, and we beheld His glory, the glory as of the only begotten of the Father, full of grace and truth"* (John 1:14). God incarnated in the person of Jesus to reveal Himself to the people He chose. He lived in the world until He had completed His mission. His mission was to take away the sin of the world and restore that which was lost which is His image in us. He offered us the opportunity to choose eternal life. He came to show us God's love and desire of having a relationship with us. Through His death, He opened the gates of heaven. When Jesus was been crucified He promised to one of the thieves next to Him that paradise was available. And Jesus said to him, "Assuredly, I say to you, today you will be with Me in Paradise" (Luke 23:43). The second revelation is written and presented to us in the Bible which was written by divine inspiration. The Holy Spirit dictated what had to be written. It teaches us everything we need in order to live with dignity in this world and to earn the ticket to the eternity. The Bible states that: "All Scripture *is* given by inspiration of God, and *is* profitable for doctrine, for reproof, for correction, for instruction in righteousness," (2 Timothy 3:16).

There is only one God, one holy book and one way to salvation. Through the Old and New Testament we read that Jesus Christ is our Savior. *"For there is one God and one Mediator between God and men, the Man Christ Jesus"* (1 Timothy 2:5). The Virgin Mary is not the mediator as many believe. This contradicts the Scriptures and we would be calling a liar to the Holy Spirit. We must be very careful here. *"Therefore I say to you, every sin and blasphemy will be forgiven men, but the blasphemy against the Spirit will not be forgiven men. Anyone who speaks a word against the Son of Man, it will be forgiven him; but whoever speaks against the Holy Spirit, it will not be forgiven him, either in this age or in the age to come"* (Matthew 12:31-32). How do we know that the Bible is the Word of God? I recommend you to ask God in Jesus Christ's name to lead you through it and you will find out. The Word of God speaks to us. In the Bible we find out the way to the Father which is Jesus Christ.

Reading the Bible was forbidden under the threat of causing mental damage. When I was a child, I never met anyone who had the Bible. The

The False Teachers   77

priests discouraged their parishioners to read the Bible. At mass they only read portions of the letters of John, Peter and Paul to certain churches and the rest of the Bible was unknown. My sister once told me that it is not necessary to read the Bible because the priest teaches you all about it. She said that only the Catholics are going to be saved, disregarding the sacrifice of Jesus on the cross. The Catholic Church distributed a book that condemns all religions that differ from Catholicism. It is very sad to know that there are millions of people in the world following that deceiving religion. The Bible totally contradicts that doctrine saying the following: *"As we have said before, so now I say again, if anyone preaches any other gospel to you than what you have received, let him be accursed"* (Galatians 1:9). The four Gospel accounts contain all the teaching of Jesus while He was in the world. Paul wrote long letters that contain everything a Christian should do to please Christ.

The Bible is a manual for the children of God. Without reading it we do not know God's will and we just do what pleases us or what others instruct us to do. I read in the Bible the Ten Commandments to my sister, and then I advised her to discharge her statues and images of those whom they have in an altar at home. She said that she would if I would destroy the Holy Bible. It is very difficult to teach people about God when they disregard the Bible. According to Catholicism the savior is not Jesus but their religion and all their fictional saints. But the Bible says: *"This is the 'stone which was rejected by you builders, which has become the chief cornerstone. Nor is there salvation in any other, for there is no other name under heaven given among men by which we must be saved"* (Acts 4:11-12). Every person is responsible for his or her own salvation. Although the person who swindles has a big responsibility on his head, it is also true that those who are deceived are not saved when they reject the truth. My dad has tried to convince me to follow the religion they taught me. All of my immediate family has alienated me since I decided to follow Jesus; they have chosen instead to follow their religion.

The priest of my hometown told my relatives I will be crazy very soon if I keep reading the Bible. The ignorance of my own people makes me very sad. It is ironic because in many ways they ignore what had been taught to them by their parents and they do what pleases them. They only do what suits them or better said what suits the devil, the one who keeps

78   Breaking Bondages

them blind. Hell is real but people prefer to ignore it. My dad cannot understand the damage he would have caused me with his advice if I had chosen to follow it. The torments of hell are horrendous. There is not and never will be worse suffering that can be compared with this torment. God shows us an example of the agonies of hell through a rich man.

> *And being in torments in Hades, he lifted up his eyes and saw Abraham afar off, and Lazarus in his bosom. "Then he cried and said, 'Father Abraham, have mercy on me, and send Lazarus that he may dip the tip of his finger in water and cool my tongue; for I am tormented in this flame.' But Abraham said, 'Son, remember that in your lifetime you received your good things, and likewise Lazarus evil things; but now he is comforted and you are tormented. And besides all this, between us and you there is a great gulf fixed, so that those who want to pass from here to you cannot, nor can those from there pass to us.' "Then he said, 'I beg you therefore, father, that you would send him to my father's house, for I have five brothers, that he may testify to them, lest they also come to this place of torment.' ²⁹ Abraham said to him, 'They have Moses and the prophets; let them hear them.' And he said, 'No, father Abraham; but if one goes to them from the dead, they will repent.' But he said to him, 'If they do not hear Moses and the prophets, neither will they be persuaded though one rise from the dead.'"*
>
> *Luke 16:23-34*

God wants everyone to have eternal life. I do not want to go to hell. I will fight against everything and everyone to secure me a place in heaven with my heavenly Father whom I love with all my heart. Not only will I fight for my salvation, but for that of all my family and friends at the expenses of my own life.

The Storms of Hell

For Tophet was established of old,
Yes, for the king it is prepared.
He has made it deep and large;
Its pyre is fire with much wood;
The breath of the Lord,
like a stream of brimstone,
Kindles it.
Isaiah 30:33

People deny hell exists but it is mentioned throughout the Bible. In the above passage we read that it was not created for people but for the devil, which is the king of the world. God does not want anyone to go to that place of torment where a fire is burning forever. We cannot conceive how hot it is. After learning this fact would you still risk to continue ignoring the truth? You may wonder how I know this. First, I do not question God's Word, and it is available for everyone to examine it. Second, because God in His infinite love is revealing His mysteries to prevent people from going to that horrible place. Many people have died and returned from the dead telling horror stories describing hell. Others have received revelations from God in dreams and visions where they have seen the horrors of hell. God reveals what He wants us to know. In the Holy Scriptures we read: "However, when He, the Spirit of truth, has come, He will guide you into all truth; for He will not speak on His own *authority*, but whatever He hears He will speak; and He will tell you things to come. He will glorify Me, for He will take of what is Mine and declare *it* to you" (John 16:13-14).

The dreams and visions are some signs of end times. " 'And it shall come to pass in the last days, says God, That I will pour out of My Spirit on all flesh; Your sons and your daughters shall prophesy, Your young men shall see visions, Your old men shall dream dreams. And on My menservants and on My maidservants. I will pour out My Spirit in those days; And they shall prophesy" (Acts 2:17-18).

All prophecies are written and God is confirming them. We are being warned of the dangers of dying without knowing the way to heaven which is Jesus. I recently read a book where one person was taken by God in the spirit to that horrible place called hell. God sustained him so he did not suffer so much while he was observing all the different chambers of hell. His experience was very traumatic. The most horrible nightmare we can ever experience left him in a state of total shock. He said that he would never have recovered from the shock without God's help. God instructed him to go around giving testimony of what he saw and experienced firsthand. When I read that book I immediately identified with him. I immediately knew that it was necessary to share that book. I read it quickly so I could pass it on to others. I also know of other people who went to the store and bought several copies to give them away. The suffering in that place was not like anyone you could imagine and we must try to avoid it at all costs. If we say that we love Jesus, we must take care of His sheep.

Chapter 11

God Speaks to us in various forms

"In the beginning was the Word, and the Word was with God, and the Word was God"

John 1:1

By reading the above quote we can conclude that what John means is that God wants to communicate his thoughts with His creation. The Spanish version instead of calling God the "Word" it calls Him the "The Verb". The verbs are action words. Through this metaphor John is telling us that Jesus is action, not a noun. God is always working as Jesus said to the Pharisees who criticized Him for healing on the Sabbath. The names He reveals to us are based in the purpose of the revelation. For example Emmanuel means God with us and Jesus in Hebrew literally means Savior. Jehovah Rapha is our healer or our doctor, Jehova Nissi is our banner of protection and love. Jehova Jireh is our provider, Jehova Raah is the pastor who leads us and keeps us safe. Jehovah Sabaoth is the Lord of Hosts, our Protector, Jehovah Shammah is the Lord who is with us everywhere for He is Omnipresent. Jehova Shalom is our perfect peace. Jehova-Tsid-Kenu means The Lord is our righteousness and our hope. The Lord uses many ways to communicate with us. He likes to whisper in our ear but our daily routines and our sins prevent us from hearing His voice. He speaks to us through the Holy Scriptures. He uses people's experiences and testimonies to break chains that bind us to the world. God is the living Word who wants to inform us that He is near to help and protect us at all times. He is working hard to help us escape from the traps of the devil if we choose Him.

The Holy Scriptures show us that God wants to have a relationship with men. Throughout the Bible we see that God speaks. His words are quoted in the four Gospel accounts by their writers. He has not only spoken, but He is still speaking every time we open the Holy Book. The voice of God is deep, free and without limits of time or space. Jesus said: "It is the Spirit who gives life; the flesh profits nothing. The words that I speak to you are spirit, and *they* are life" (John 6:63). He injects energy and positive changes to our lives when He speaks to us. In the Bible we find all the instructions to have successful lives according to God's will. God continuously speaks to us through nature as well; the world is full of his voice. He has created a perfect balance. He made the trees to purify the oxygen that mankind breathes. There is interdependence between the two, the man breathes what trees exhale and trees inhale what man exhales. The following biblical passage explains that it is ignorance to deny God's existence. "For since the creation of the world His invisible *attributes* are clearly seen, being understood by the things that are made, *even* His eternal power and Godhead, so that they are without excuse," *(Romans 1:20)*.

We must learn to recognize the voice of God. All that happens in our lives is orchestrated by God who is in control of the world. With the power of His word He created the universe. He just said let it be and it happened. The Word of God either written or spoken is the divine energy that fills everything with living power. The voice of God is the most powerful energy in the universe. All energy is derived from what God had said. Even the Bible

God Speaks to us in various forms   83

itself has that energy locked within its pages. When we read it, we can feel that God is leading us through His Word. Many times while reading it we clearly feel that certain messages are directly aimed at us. He answers our questions, clarifies our doubts and comforts us in our sorrows. The Lord also speaks to us through people close to us or even through the media. Other times He sends His angels to give us messages and there are times when He speaks loud and clear directly to us without any intermediaries.

God has revealed Himself to many people through the ages. He spoke to Abraham from man to man. He spoke to Moses from a burning bush. The Israelites saw a cloud that led them during the day and a pillar of fire at night. They saw great wonders during their exodus to the Promised Land. Walking through the middle of the Red Sea and the Jordan River are some of the wonders they experienced from firsthand. When they were thirsty, the water came out of the rocks and the manna came down from heaven to feed them when they were hungry. Other people have also been very privileged. The Lord used them to reveal His plans hundreds of years before He came. The prophets Isaiah, Jeremiah, Ezekiel, Daniel and many others received amazing revelations from the Lord. God used them to prepare the way for His first and second coming revealing to them things that would happen before the end. The plan of salvation was revealed thousands of years before the Lord came. When Jacob blessed and prophesied for his children, he received divine revelations about them. The prophecies about two of his sons Judah and Joseph were both fulfilled according to the scriptures. Knowing our Heavenly Father I am sure that the prophecy about the other children are also fulfilled but if they are not recorded I will not mention them. Joseph saved his family from a famine because God revealed to him in a dream what was to come. God also gave him wisdom and all means to meet the needs of the people of Egypt. Joseph saved them from a physical starvation or gave them the salvation of the body. The prophecy about Judah said that the scepter would never be taken away from him until the coming of He who deserves all the tributes of the entire universe. The Lord was revealing that an eternal king was coming to the earth. This is of course a reference to Jesus Christ. Jesus is a descendant of the tribe of Judah and the Lord revealed it to Jacob thousands of years before His coming (Gen.49:9-12).

84   Breaking Bondages

In the last years, it is common to hear people speaking about their dreams. I want to humbly share some of my dreams, which are consistent with what God told the prophets about the end times. I want to give God the glory He deserves. It is written that in the last times young people would prophesy and elders will have dreams (Joel 2:28). God reveals His mysteries for the sake of His kingdom. The Lord Jesus Christ has been very generous with me who has been one of the worst sinners. I have offended my heavenly Father greatly. Through His infinite love He has forgiven me and allowed me to call Him Father. The Bible says that a thankful heart receives revelation from God who gives us power and wisdom (Daniel 2:23). God reveals His mysteries because He wants us to share them with others for the edification of the church (2 Peter 1:20). The church is the body of Christ and He wants to have a healthy one.

God makes clear our call!

We were all created with a purpose. When we are ready to hear the voice of God, He reveals to us our call. To hear God we must acknowledge His existence and seek Him. I received my call a few months after I recognized that He was the only one that could help me during a huge trial. He called me by my name through an audible voice. It was a Saturday morning before I got up from my bed. While lying half-awake I heard something that confused me for several months. Before I heard God's voice, I heard bizarre noises that sounded as if there were a multitude of people gathered. I also overheard when a man would say something to each of the people who were waiting their turn in line for something. For a moment I listened as each person is commended something. After a while I realized that I was in that line. When my turn came, the voice of an old man told me something that left me very confused. His voice was strong and spoke in English with a small accent to pronounce my name. He said "Maria you have a big back up". The message confused me and I wondered who had told me that. I had never heard that God speaks to people as He did it in the Old Testament time. All the people

I knew then were religious who never had supernatural manifestations of God's presence. Various months passed before I found out that it was my heavenly Father who spoke to me. I also understand why He spoke to me in English instead of in Spanish. He used a co-worker to witness me about the gospel and she does not speak much Spanish. When I talked to her about what I had heard she quickly told me that it was the Lord of hosts.

When I found out that the Lord had spoken to me more questions arose. What was the Lord commanding me? I started to ask Him directly to explain to me what He meant. One day while reading the Scriptures I found the answer. I read two versus that clarified any doubt about God's call for me. The Scripture says: *"I have commanded My sanctified ones; I have also called My mighty ones for My anger—Those who rejoice in My exaltation." The noise of a multitude in the mountains, Like that of many people! A tumultuous noise of the kingdoms of nations gathered together! The Lord of hosts musters. The army for battle"* (Isaiah 13:3-4).

God was telling me that I am a soldier and that I have a great support. The Lord was calling His warriors to send them to fight in the final battle, or the day of his wrath. The message here seems to indicate that the day of his wrath is near. God is calling brave people who dare to fight against the enemy for the salvation of many souls before it's too late. I sincerely wish to fulfill the purpose for which I was called. What I want the most in the world is to take care of the sheep of my father and always do His will.

The Lord is now continuously communicating with us through dreams. Three years later, through a dream the Lord gave me another message revealing that the wrath of God is coming upon the world. I saw myself in a transparent tent full of people worshiping God with wind musical instruments. The tent was settled in a desert surrounded by many smaller tents. Although the musicians were from different nationalities, they all wore orange robes as the Tibetan monks. There were people of all ages and races. I was among the attendees of that tabernacle. The tabernacle attracted famous reporters who were allowed to enter it to worship too. A man walked to the altar and asked us to sing a hymn from the book of Isaiah. I opened my Bible and looked for that song to worship as well. In the morning when I woke up the dream images were vivid in my mind, but

86   Breaking Bondages

I could not remember the biblical cite. I prayed to the Lord to remind me that biblical cite. Moments later I opened the Bible and found the hymn we were singing in the dream. It goes like this: "Come, my people, enter your chambers, And shut your doors behind you; Hide yourself, as it were, for a little moment, Until the indignation is past. For behold, the Lord comes out of His place to punish the inhabitants of the earth for their iniquity; the earth will also disclose her blood, And will no more cover her slain." (Isaiah 26:20-21). I understand that the transparent tent means an invisible barrier that separates us from the world. I think that God wants us to live our life similar to that of the monks who consecrate their lives to their religion. But He does not want us isolated from the world in order to witness to them. We should be praising God in front of people to model for the world. We must keep our doors closed to the worldly desires in order to escape the wrath of God. The Lord has promised to protect us during the hour of trial that will affect the whole world. "Because you have kept My command to persevere, I also will keep you from the hour of trial which shall come upon the whole world, to test those who dwell on the earth" (Revelation 3:10).

Once again I heard God's voice with another audible message. A conversation woke me and I got up because I heard they were referring to me. Someone was accusing me of something that I did not understand. I clearly heard when a man responded to another person "She's honest, she's honest". In the Bible we read that the devil is always accusing us with the Lord (Rev. 12:10). I think that is what I heard. Satan was the one accusing me of doing wrong deeds. Satan always accuses us to God but the Holy Spirit searches our hearts and knows if we are sincere or not. Why did He say twice that I was honest? In the scriptures Jesus always repeated things twice for clarification. I am so blessed to be so loved by God. But He loves us all. Recently I heard the same voice one more time. A man told me that my life would be like Joshua's, despite my children. Joshua's life was entirely guided by the Holy Spirit who always held his hand and that's what I desire the most. He was chosen by the Lord God as Moses' successor and people recognized him as such. In addition, Joshua was responsible for dividing the land along with Eleazar son of Aaron (Numbers 27:18-23). When Moses died, God renewed Joshua and reminded him of the promise of the land of

Canaan, where Joshua should conquer. God commanded him to cross the Jordan River to reach the Promised Land. The Ark of the Covenant was placed in the bed of the River to divide the water (Joshua 3). Joshua defeated an alliance of five kings. They intended to attack the Gibeonites who helped the Israelites when God held the sun in the middle of the sky (Joshua 10:13). Joshua and his people served the Lord through several generations and that is my goal. I want to help people cross the river to reach the New Jerusalem.

Spiritual Warfare

For we do not wrestle against flesh and blood, but against principalities, against powers, against the rulers of the darkness of this age, against spiritual hosts of wickedness in the heavenly places.

Ephesians 6:12

During the time of Moses and Joshua, the wars to reach the Promised Land were physical. They faced seven pagan tribes living in the Promised Land. Our wars now to get to heaven are spiritual. We must fight in the spiritual realm against all sorts of demons among which stand out the demons of religion, fornication, idolatry, pornography, love of money, etc. We face evil spirits every time we try to bring the truth to our families and friends. Our own family persecutes us when we decide to follow Christ. We are reviled by our coworkers and even at church where we expect to be understood. My dad and my brothers call me crazy because I read the Bible. No one can stop me because the Lord always comforts me. I know that one day, sooner or later, my Lord will remove the blindfold from them to let them see the light. I have learned that even in the darkest moments of our life the Lord gives us peace and comfort. He heals our wounds and when we least expect it they are cured. God promised in His Word to help us and He will: "'Call to Me, and I will answer you, and show you great and mighty things, which you do not know'" (Jeremiah 33:3).

True Christians are always enduring difficult trials. My life is not easy at home with four worldly children. I try to be a good mother but it is difficult to compete with all the temptations our children are exposed to on an everyday basis. Schools and society in general are full of danger. Drugs abound and the vice dens have multiplied. Only the peace of God can help us to overcome our fears. Thanks to my God I have a heart that is rock solid. After I pray and leave my children in God's hands, I peacefully go to sleep. The Word of God says that we do not gain anything with worrying. It advises us to leave our battles to the Lord that He would fight them. Just as He fought Joshua's battles, He will fight ours as well if we trust in Him. God is amazing. He surprises me. I find it amusing to see that often times He responds when I do not even ask. He knows our needs and tries to honor us. He is so lovely; I have no words to express my gratitude to Him for all He does for me and my family every day. I see His hand in everything I do. He makes my life much easier. When I teach He plans my lessons and teaches my classes. In my job as dean, I daily see His unconditional support. With His support I escape many headaches. Working with the youth these days is very difficult. Understanding and supporting their views is a challenge. The Bible studies I organize are led by Him as well as my own my life.

God is always trying to please us although we do not deserve it. This testimony involves one of my children. He has been stubborn and denies that God exists. He strongly argues his philosophy regarding life and sometime makes rude comments about my Creator. God knows my son speaks in ignorance and does not take it into account. His face changes when he curses against God. It is obvious that Satan is using him to blaspheme against God. I raise my hands in prayer and within minutes he forgets what he was saying. Whenever he speaks ill of my heavenly Father I ask God to forgive him. I rebuke the evil forces that use him to disrespect my God. When Lucifer goes away, he transforms himself into a sweet boy. One day right after a harsh moment of disagreement, I was surprised by what he said. While in the car with my other children, he acknowledged that he believes in God. He even shared that he conveys that to his friends. He recognizes that nothing bad has happened to him because his mother prays to God for his protection. He apparently sees a vision where he sees and hears me kneeling and praying. God in His infinite love revealed to him the power of prayer and how much He loves him. Every time the devil assaults him, he goes against me. One day he said that he would rather die than read this book and repeated it several times with hatred. I asked him to get out of my bedroom and started to pray for him. A few minutes later he returned to tell me that he was going to read it. His opposition against this book encouraged me even more to finish and publish it. I realized that Satan does not want me to finish it, so that people can read it. I have had so many obstacles. In Mexico they printed it completely wrong, but that contributed to my desire to publish it regardless.

Chapter 12

God Opens and Closes Doors

*"The wind blows wherever it pleases. You hear its sound,
but cannot tell where it comes from or where it goes. So is everyone
who is born of the Spirit.*

John 3:8

The life of every true Christian is moved by the Holy Spirit. God moved me to work in a different school because He wanted me to open a Christian club at that campus. I was very comfortable in my former school but as a servant of the Lord I had to obey and follow Him. I tried to start the club during the lunch recess but I did not know what to do. Soon the Lord sent me some students to start it. The club opened with six students and two months later it had over thirty students. They met twice a week to learn the Word of God and to worship Him. The club attracted other Christian teachers as well and we moved it to accommodate it to the schedule of the students. As the club was growing, problems started to arise. The devil was jealous that we worshipped God in that place that used to be just for him. Adults started to preach instead of the children as it should

92   Breaking Bondages

be done at school. The founders of the club and I were worried about the doctrines they were preaching. When the kids preached the adults criticized and discouraged them. I was displaced as the sponsor by a person I had invited to participate. I suggested a collective fasting with the founders to ask God for direction in this situation. The message taught at the last meeting troubled us. We prayed to the Father not to permit topics that would cause division and confusion among the attendees. The preacher had planned to speak about the concerned topic but the time did not allow him. He promised to continue with it the next week. On the way to my classroom I told one of the students that many things could happen in a week, and they did. There were a series of sermons that did not happen because the Lord heard our prayers. The club fell apart two days later and I was blamed for it. I was a victim of harassment and insults by several members of the club including those that called themselves pastors. Most of the adults and various students stayed away from me except for the club founders which were the six students sent by the Lord to start the club. For a moment they were confused by all the comments but did not fall for it. The test was hard but we passed it because the Lord was there with us.

I was persecuted by people who called themselves Christians. They accused me of teaching a false doctrine based solely on dreams, visions and emotions. I rarely preach in the Christian club so this was just a lie to damage my reputation. They wrote on the doorway of my classroom the word "Arc". I was compared to Joan of Arc which is an honor for me but that was not their intention. Joan of Arc was captured and tried by an ecclesiastical court accused of witchcraft, arguing that the voices she heard came from the devil. She reaffirmed the divine origin of the voices she had heard, so she was condemned to the stake, and was executed on May 30th, 1431.

The adults involved tried to start the club again. They chose a different sponsor disregarding God's will. My classroom was not an option for them but they wanted me to support them. They could not do anything against God's plans. God comforted me when I was sad. One day I clearly heard when He told me that they were not fighting against me but against Him and that they would not win. Most of the students refused to follow them and finally they gave up. A few weeks later the Lord again opened the club in my classroom. This time He sent more people to the worship team and the doors have never been closed again. Our Father has now given us an auditorium for our gathering during the student's lunchtime. God removed all the barriers and sent great pillars to support the group. Glory be to God. Hallelujah!

True Christians are those who are born again and live a life devoted to God. The lives of these Christians are guided by the Holy Spirit to where the needs are. These people are mistreated and humiliated just because they decided to serve God. They call us irrational because we do not think like most people we know. People despise and judge us when we try to witness about Jesus. We are constantly moving from one place to another and few understand it. Persecution comes from our own family and the people at church. We are called unstable and even carnal. Jesus told Nicodemus that the born again people are like the wind; we do not know where we come from or where we are going. But wherever we are, we feel peace because God is with us. One day I climbed a mountain near my house trying to find a good place to talk to God. I prayed for a while expecting to feel a special presence of God. I did not sense anything special so sadly started to descend. As I was walking down the hill I heard the voice of the Holy Spirit recommending me to start fasting to be more sensitive to God's voice. That same day I started a 21 day fast to seek the favor of God in my ministry. I wanted to start a Spanish service at the church where I was an associate pastor. I did not receive the necessary support from the senior pastor. During those twenty-one days the Lord made big changes in my ministry. The door in my congregation was completely closed but God opened another larger door. The school where I work allowed us to use a hall for free to have our church. Now we are reaching not only the students but also their parents as well as the people who live in that community. God has provided everything we needed to perform the job he assigned. The best thing of all is that we do not need to pay for anything because this is His business and He in control. Glory to God!

Chapter 13

Divine Revelations through Dreams

Then he said, "Hear My words: If there is a prophet among you, I the Lord MAKE MYSELF KNOWN TO HIM IN VISION; I SPEAK TO HIM IN A DREAM.

Numbers 12:6

In the above passage God is revealing to us the way He speaks to the prophets. The Holy Scriptures said that in the last days the young people would prophesy and the elderly would have dreams (Acts 2:17). Lately it is very common to hear people speaking about dreams and visions. The Lord is communicating with us more and more revealing His plans. In addition to hearing the voice of God, I've also had dreams where He has revealed prophecies written in the Scriptures. While we sleep, He reveals to us His mysteries. He is preparing us to be ready for His second coming and for the trials that are coming upon the whole world. He does not want to catch us asleep and unprepared. We know that we are living in the last days because all the prophecies are being fulfilled. The Lord comforts us while we sleep. Many of the messages I receive have to do with my family to give me the peace I need. Many others serve to encourage me to continue in my struggle against the enemy to win souls for my God. When I have one of those dreams I pray to God to reveal me the meaning in order to serve Him the way He wants. I want to share some of the dreams trying to please my Lord. The dreams that I narrate below are somewhat confusing. With the Lord's help we will be able to understand them to decipher the messages He is sending to His church.

The beast dressed in blue, white and red

This terrifying dream disturbed me for weeks. I was walking towards the entrance of a mall when a children's apparel clothing store caught my attention. This establishment sold only blue denim clothing for children. I entered the store and grabbed a pair of shorts to see them. I was observing them intending to buy when I saw a beast walking towards me. Her arrogance told me that she was the owner of the shop and of the mall. The beast I saw was half donkey and half woman. She was dressed in the colors of the American flag red white and blue. When I told her I wanted to buy those shorts, she told me to wait in a very rude manner. She looked at me with hatred in her face. She made me feel as if I was the most despised person. Since I do not like to wait I replied that I had no time to wait. Her reaction to my answer was blunt and menacing. She said: "You will see if you do not have time." She strode out of the store stirring her strange body. She entered the mall, leaving me with the impression that someone would come to take care of me. Her reaction scared me so bad. I immediately put the shorts down and ran out to hide. At that moment I realized that she was a very powerful person. I knew that she went in search of her guards to send them to kill me. I thought of changing my clothes so they could not recognize me. I don't remember if I did change or not. I just remember that I ran as fast as I could uphill and walked into an orchard. When I thought I was safe I turned

Divine Revelations through Dreams   97

back to see if I was being chased. Very surprised I saw that two Roman soldiers dressed in robes were coming towards me. Trying to escape I decided to lie down in a ditch so they would not see me. As I lied down I felt that I was being observed and that there was no hope for me. Nothing could be done to escape since they were directed by a spiritual force which guided them exactly to where I was. I saw them approaching me raising two lances at once to kill me. As I lay waiting for the inevitable attack that would take away my life, I looked up to the sky seeking for divine assistance. I immediately sensed the presence of someone standing behind me. I could only see two beautiful hands dressed in white sleeves. I saw the motion of the hands covering me with a blanket so I would not be seen by the soldiers. The soldiers passed by me confused because they could not find me where they had just seen me a moment ago. After the soldiers left, I got up and looked around. I noticed that the trees of the garden had flowers of blue, red and white like the clothes of the beast. Although this dream is hard to understand, a thing I am sure of is that the hands that covered me where some holy hands like the ones of my heavenly Father.

For God there are not coincidences. One day I could not go to work because I was feeling ill, I turned on the television and found out details that I associated with my dream. A theologian and eschatologist in a television show explained some of the prophecies in Revelation 13. After hearing that explanation I was able to understand some points in my dream. He spoke about two beasts, one more powerful than the other. The one in my dream seems to be the beast that comes out of the water. The beast in my dream is an anti-Christian system supported by the most powerful country in the world. The beast in John's vision has the appearance of different animals and received authority and power directly from the dragon, which is Satan. The powerful beast in my dream was formed by two symbolic parts. The Holy Scriptures speak of a woman when referring to the church. In the United States, the Democratic Party the actual president belongs to is represented by a donkey. The beast I saw combines two powers together, the political and the religious. The religious power is the woman's head, and the political one is the donkey's body and they work in agreement. The flowers in the orchard and the dress of the beast all had the colors of the United States flag. All of these details show that this nation is part of the anti-Christian system. I do not know what role I play there, nor why the beast tried to kill me as soon as she recognized me. It seems like I represent a risk to the plans of the anti-Christian system. The chasing and the lancers represent the persecution I will endure in this nation. God showed me in this dream that I should trust him regardless of the circumstances. According with the Bible, the beast I dreamt is also known as the Antichrist. I cannot afford to make more assumptions because I fear to offend my Holy Father. Just want to wait until He gives me the right explanation if that is His will.

Five years later I dreamt of another similar beast. At first sight she looked like a pregnant woman with an extremely long belly. I approached her because she was a girl from my hometown that I have not seen for more than thirty years. She was driving a chariot and stopped to pick up some people by the street where I was passing by. One of the people was her father who died when I was little. I asked her if she could take me too but she said that she was taking people to a party and refused. As she moved forward I could see that four donkey legs were moving from under her elongated belly. What at first looked as the belly of a pregnant woman ended up being the body of a donkey. I stared at it as it departed and saw that the people she was carrying were people dressed as angels. The weird woman with donkey legs was pulling a religious float. After the chariot left, I walked up the hill to wait for a bus to take me to an unknown destination. When I reached the top of the hill where the road was I noticed my dress was all ripped by hidden thorns.

Discerning this dream seems easy. The Lord knows the truth. The pregnant woman with a huge stomach could represent a coming event of great magnitude. The woman itself depicts a church but her hidden traits tell us that it is a hypocritical one. The woman is the beast mentioned in the Revelation thirteen. The girl from my hometown reveals that the church embodied by the woman is the one I know since I was little. Catholicism is the religion I left when I met the Lord Jesus. The woman's father is already dead for a long time, he represents the fate of that church's followers. Jesus is the life; the devil is the death and the beast is leading people to it. The people dressed as angels could represent all the fake Christians that follow that beast led by the ecumenical movement.

The woman in the underground village

In this dream I had a negative encounter with another powerful woman. An employment agent pursued me to go for a job interview with an important person. The agency was responsible for finding a well-qualified person to perform a distinctive task. I was not interested in that position that was apparently in a secret company or very important organization. The same agent picked me up from my house and took me to the interview since he was sure to have the right person. We entered a subway to find a village with many offices and narrow streets. I saw several known people walking in the streets but they ignored me although they knew me. One boy greeted me very afraid of being seen and quickly disappeared. The agent and I waited standing on one of the streets for a few minutes. After a short time waiting, the person that was going to interview me walked towards us. An entourage escorted her. She wore a white dress with gold designs and a belt and gold shoes as well. The agent was very excited and confident that he had the right person for that position. He introduced me as soon as she arrived. As I shook her hand to greet her and say my name she recognized me. As soon as she heard my name, she withdrew her hand and turned her face away showing a horrible gesture of disapproval. I politely tried to convince her of my qualifications and abilities. She looked at me again with disgust and walked away from us very upset.

We did not understand the reaction of the woman. When she was gone, I naively asked the agent if I was going to be employed. The agent still confused replied to me that she hated me. What I understand about this dream is that this woman could be a system of organized religion. Today, the enemy leads many churches and religions. A powerful organization that pretends to be holy hates me because I am trying to expose her lies. Their business needs someone with my qualifications to be manipulated by the organization. The agent knew me and he thought that I was the person required by his client. He was deceived by them as there are millions of people in the world who lead others to their church instead of leading them to Jesus. The woman cannot stand to be near a godly person. Her dress color mimics the color of the clothes that Jesus wears in the vision of John in the Isle of Patmos (Rev.

1:13). By the woman's outfit I can deduce that it is an apostate church. It is a church that claims to be holy but hides the truth, which could be represented by the subway and the underground village. The subway could also represent a secret society that is led by a person who claims to be holy but is just a false prophet. In various biblical messages we can see that God shows women to refer to religions as well as cities. Perhaps one day our heavenly Father would reveal the meaning of this other dream.

Women in labor

In this dream I heard the loud screaming of a woman in excruciating pain. I thought she was dying. I looked around for her concerned about the screams. I was in an unknown place. After a while I sat down then I saw a lady with a big and pointy belly, pass by me. She was about to give birth to a child. The dreams of women about to give birth have been repeated several times. Another time I dreamt several women in a village were all pregnant. In another dream I saw three pregnant women, two were having baby girls and a third was having a boy. But all three were very advanced in pregnancy. The Bible uses the analogy of women about to give birth to tell us that one or more events are about to happen. The number of pregnant women may indicate that there will be the same amount of new events occurring soon. There are several events to come according to Bible prophecy. We now are expecting two great ones. One is the revealing of the Antichrist who should be done before the greatest event the Christian people is waiting for. The other is our Lord Jesus Christ descending from the clouds to gather His church. These two could be very close and God wants us to know and be prepared. The apostle Paul wrote a letter to the church in Thessalonica clarifying any doubts as seen in the following quote. "…not to be soon shaken in mind or troubled, either by spirit or by word or by letter, as if from us, as though the day of Christ had come. Let no one deceive you by any means; for *that Day will not come* unless the falling away comes first, and the man of sin is revealed, the son of perdition," (2 Thessalonians 2:2-3).

Divine Revelations through Dreams   101

In one dream three different boys wanted to give us important information. One by one they came and the last would mourn when my husband told him that he did not want to hear them. I called him by his name which I remember was Mark and I encouraged him to tell me all he knew. He then began to pray with tears in his eyes and told me that the Lord was coming soon. He was very distressed because people did not care about such an important event. He was terrified because he knew the things that will be happening when Jesus comes to judge the world and the people are not prepared.

God has also revealed me pieces of information about an antichristian system in two different dreams. In the first one I saw a very huge white newborn child. I learned that this baby was from Russia. In the other dream the images were more vivid. I went to visit a family that I knew for years. Their house looked empty because of its size. It looked like a huge warehouse. There was a big man babysitting a huge baby in an incubator. The incubator was made of a transparent glass tub, and it was covered with water halfway. The baby was enormous despite being born premature. He was white and chunky. The baby was lying happily in the water. The man who took care of him placed a pillow to lift the baby's head so that way he could breathe. The bizarre thing is that the big baby would budge from his position to lay with his head under the water. The man fixed the pillow under his head every time the baby pushed it away. It seemed like he preferred to stay with his head submerged under the water. As if he did not need to breathe. The man picked up the baby and sat him in his lap to feed him. I could not stop contemplating that strange baby. Right before the man placed the bottle in the baby's mouth to feed him, the baby turned to me. His face was very similar to that of Chucky the evil doll from the movie. He gave me a scary and threatening look and laughed diabolically. I ran scared towards the exit. I escaped through the door without opening it. I did not need to open the door because I was in the spirit when I was showed that enormous baby. We see here again the beast that comes from the water. The water represents the world. The beast is in the incubator until it is well developed.

The Three Dragons

The Bible speaks of a huge dragon, which was cast down to the ground. The dragon dragged with him the third part of the stars (Revelation 12:4). The dragon referred to here is Satan himself when he rebelled against God. As an imitator of God he has prepared two strong allies to work together. Its sole purpose is to deceive both big and small men. The Holy Trinity consists of the Father, Word and Holy Spirit (I John 5:7-8). The devil has his diabolical dumbbell which is formed by him, the antichrist and the false prophet. The Word of God describes the allies of Satan as two mighty beasts (Revelation 13). In a dream, I saw the silhouette of three different size dragons. All three were huge. Their silhouettes in the water covered the surface of a large channel. The fact they were revealed in shadows could mean these mighty beasts are already among us but are disguised. They have not yet manifested themselves in public because God has not allowed it. The Holy Scriptures tells us that something is stopping that for now (2 Thessalonians 2:6). God knows what He is doing.

The four horses of the Apocalypse

In this dream I was driving along a path next to a stream with several people. One of them was my cousin with whom I spent most of my childhood. We were trying to go to a certain village. Someone told me that the travel distance to get there was twenty-three miles. We were walking with great difficulty because the path merged with the stream and walking in water is not easy. We wanted to drive a car but could not. Sometimes we pushed it and other time we carried it. I decided to go ahead of the people who were with me. I wanted to look over to see if the road was going to take us to our destination. I soon realized that the road was not going to take us anywhere. The road was closed a little ahead of where I had left my cousin and the others. Closing the road was a high fence of barbed wire. The wires were reinforced and close to each another as well as the posts supporting them.

Divine Revelations through Dreams   103

I observed the fence trying to find a way to cross by, when suddenly I saw a huge reddish horse running in my direction. It was an untamed and very strong horse that looked threatening.

I stayed paralyzed with fear because there was nothing I could do to prevent anything that horse could do to me. The horse passed near me but did not see me. It ran towards the fence, crossed it without any difficulty and went forward. Frightened, I saw it approach a big semi-truck parked by the roadside. The truck was high but the horse was also huge and could reach the top of the truck. I saw how the horse broke the window. He opened his muzzle and bit the window tearing it apart as if it was a piece of paper. I heard the moaning of a scared person who was inside the truck cab unable to react. This horse seemed uncontrollable and prepared to kill.

This horrible dream stayed in my mind for several days. I could not understand why a horse behaved like that when horses are not usually harmful. Weeks later while I was getting ready to go to work I turned on the TV to hear the weather reports. By accident I turned on the TV to a Christian channel. To my surprise at the time a theologian was speaking about the horses in the book of Revelation. He talked about the prophecy of the four horses coming out when one of the seals was opened. I had read that book but I did not understand it because I was not led by the Holy Spirit. This person explained that the Lamb opened the seals and from there came up four horses of different colors. Each horse symbolizes something. The first is white and that is mounted by the antichrist who wants to imitate Jesus. It is written that Jesus will come riding a white horse as we see it in this passage. *"I saw heaven opened, and behold a white horse. Its rider is called Faithful and True. With justice he judges and makes war. His eyes are like blazing fire, and his head are many crowns. Has a name written that no one knows except him"* (Rev. 19:11-12). The second one is reddish or russet and that was given power to take peace from the world and make war. The third is black and that was empowered to bring famine and pestilence. Finally the pale one brings with it a lot death. The horse I saw was red exactly as described in this revelation, furious and uncontrollable (Rev. 6:1-8). It seems clear that we are now living in the end times mentioned in the book of Revelation. The four horses are trials sent to the world and we are now enduring them.

104   Breaking Bondages

Months later I dreamed about another horse. This was red as blood, and it was also scary. This dream began in a river where I was washing clothes. I washed many of my husband's shirts and set them on a rock sticking up out of the water. My husband came over to examine them. In doing so some shirts fell overboard and the current took them away. The river entered through a tunnel near the spot where I was doing laundry. The water opened a hole in the wall of the tunnel to get into the ground. My two sons, my husband and I followed the river trying to catch the shirts before they went through the hole. The shirts went down the hole in the wall. We tried to reach them with a stick but we failed. As we approached the tunnel entrance I noticed that it was a secret meeting place. There was a large congregation of Asian people. They encouraged us to enter the hole to reach the shirts. The hole took us to another large but dark underground tunnel. It seemed like a huge deserted and wet cavern. The only light that came in went through the hole where the river entered it. We could barely see anything inside the cavern and suddenly we had in front of us a dark red furious horse. This horse also resembled a dragon. It was a beast that guarded the cavern and came to attack us. We tried to run away from it but there was another barbed wire fence. Risking ripping our flesh, we dragged our bodies under the fence to escape the ferocious animal. With great difficulty we managed to cross under the fence. On the other side of the fence, the river ran in a deep canyon with sharp rocks on the shore. The horse chased us as we ran as fast as we could.

We were running along the river over the dangerous cliff with sharp rocks led by a powerful force that protected us. The horse was right behind us but never reached us because God sent His angels to help us to run as if we were on a flat track. I could sense an incredible strength that pushed us to run faster than the horse. I felt relieved when we finally reached the exit of the underground place. The horse could not come to the light and that was our salvation. When we were out of danger, I sat down to rest because I was exhausted and scared. As I sat down trying to recover from the fright we endured, four small winged beings approached me. They told me to call the other three people to come and sit near. My husband and my kids came and sat near us. Each one of the little beings was transformed into young, smiling and friendly boys. The friendly boys sat next to each of us and began to make us laugh to help us forget the bad moments that had just passed. After a while we were all laughing happily as if nothing had happened. This is the second dream of red horses. According to the revelation given to John on the isle of Patmos the red horse will bring war. This dream could mean that we are close to some war and it seems to be initiated by an Asian country. The people I saw in the secret meeting inside the tunnel had Asian physical traits. They had control over the cellar where the dark red horse was locked. When I discerned what I just said, I asked my Holy Father to tell me what He wanted me to do with respect to this message. The Holy Spirit whispered to me I should pray for peace in the world. I also understood my family will be persecuted by the forces of darkness for a while but the light will come eventually.

I saw another horse in my dreams. This one occurred shortly before the outbreak of the swine flu epidemic in the world. A big yellow pale horse appeared at the entrance of a huge establishment that looks like an auditorium. The horse was moving forward as if to enter and then slowly backed up to reenter the doorway again. Each time it moved its legs his hooves would resonate strongly throughout. I associated this dream with another I had a few days earlier where two women and I were just about to give birth. I am from Mexico and my unborn baby was a girl. In my dreams the pregnant woman symbolizes something is about to happen somewhere. According to the Holy Scriptures, the pale horse has the power to bring death to the world. The epidemic started in Mexico and the events were heard around the world. The horse enters a place and stops and re-enters and stops again strangely. The pale horse according to the book of Revelation represents death. There were several deaths caused by the epidemic but it was more the alarm than the consequences. Only God knows the truth of everything.

The girl standing in the water

I dreamt I was walking through a narrow path to go to a river. When I reached the edge I spotted a girl standing under the water completely clothed and wearing shoes. Although the water passed beyond her head, she was calm. When I saw her submerged in the water unable to breathe I rushed into the water trying to save her. I reached down and took her by the waist to bring her to the surface. What I saw at that moment was weird. I pulled the girl out of the water but she struggled trying to go back. She felt slimy as she slipped out of my hands to go back into the water. I tried several times but she insisted on staying in the water. She reacted like a fish that needs water to live. While struggling with the girl I heard the noise of rushing waters, and I knew that a flood was already near. I had to hurry out of the water before the current dragged us both away. The noise of the rushing waters woke me up. I got up to go to the bathroom and went back to bed. When I closed my eyes I felt as if my head had turned around, then I saw myself flying at a high speed. While flying I watched the road but the speed distorted the shapes. I could just see dark gray clouds passing rapidly. The trip lasted about two minutes.

I arrived to my uncle's house in my hometown fifteen hundred miles away from home. I walked through the door without opening it. Upon entering I saw a man without shirt sitting next to the door. There were other people in the hallway but I did not know who they were. Sitting in front of a man whom I could only see his body, was a woman reading him a book. I did not understand what she was reading. My dream ended there. During the dream I learned that the man sitting in the chair was my uncle and that the woman was his daughter. I also learned that the woman and the girl from the past dream were the same person. She was no longer a little girl here but instead the adult she is today. In the morning when I woke up I kept thinking about the spiritual journey. I asked God for discernment and realized that the girl who was drowning in the creek was my cousin. This cousin one day saved me from drowning in a ten-foot deep pool. Now the Lord was giving me the opportunity to repay the favor by helping her escape the fires of hell. She is one of those people who believe that their religion is going to save her. Most people today could not survive under water for more than three minutes. She was calm like a fish or amphibian living in the water. The Lord showed me that this girl was drowning without knowing it and He wants to save her. The growing noise of water that came close indicates that there is not time to waste. The day of the Lord is coming in full force such as a

Divine Revelations through Dreams   107

large river that sweeps everything away. In the dream I understood that the
current would take us both. This tells me that we must hurry to share the
gospel of the Lord to save as many people as possible in accordance with the
will of God (Mat. 28:19).

From the spiritual trip to my hometown I understood if my cousin knew
the truth, she could teach it to her dad and to other family members. Most of
my family rejects the Word of God. She has two sisters who already received
Jesus Christ in their lives. The next day after my dream, I called her and
shared the dream with her. I recommended that she read the Scriptures; she
assured me she would do it. I called twice that same week to convince her to
seek the truth and she told me she was already reading the Bible. I thought
about visiting her home but did not think I would have time to do so. She
lives about three hours away from my house. One weekend we planned a trip
to see the giant sequoia trees in a park of California. We made reservations
at a hotel in a town near the park. I knew she lived in a town near that area
but I did not figure she lived two blocks away from the hotel where we would
stay. I called and asked if she knew the town where I was spending the night.
To my surprise, she said that she lives in that town. Her home was two blocks
away from our hotel room. She invited us to eat and we happily accepted the
invitation. I went over with the intention to share the gospel of Jesus with her.
Sadly, but it is the truth, when she heard me mention the subject, she locked
herself in the bathroom to ignore the conversation. I wanted to be cautious
but her husband began to speak to us about the Word. Gladly we proceeded
on the same subject because we love it. The next day she went with us to see
the sequoias but avoided talking to me at all costs. She behaved so strange
as if someone or something banned her from getting near me. Perhaps it
was God who did not want me to get so close to her. Perhaps I was not well
prepared to face the demons that blocked her understanding. I tried to bring
the truth to her because my desire is to be obedient to my heavenly Father.
Her husband advised me not to throw my pearls to the swine for he already
knew her stiffness. He reminded me that God does not want anyone coming
to Him by force. He wants us to follow Him by choice. He will be happy to
receive us in His holy kingdom if we decide so.

The village by the sea

In this dream I saw myself teaching about the Word of God. I was in a village near the sea and I saw when the edge of the beach began to slide down in the water. The houses were slowly collapsing. I managed to escape and ran towards the other side of village. Sea waves came dragging people into the water. I was amazed when I saw people walking very serene in the water. The water covered them up to their eyes and I worried about them. I knew they were drowning helplessly and wanted to rescue them but they ignored me. What I understood from this dream is that God compares people who are deceived by their religion with people who live tranquilly under the water. Religion is like a strong wave or a river that carries people to a place where it is impossible to escape without God's help. Religions do not teach us to die to live in Christ. We live comfortably believing the devil's lies telling us not to worry. God shows drowning people to us who are out of the water, so we can hurry to rescue them before it is too late. The rescue is done with prayer and evangelism for the people He sends to us.

The above interpretation is consistent with a dream one of my sisters had. I have tried to convince her that the only one who can save her is our Lord Jesus Christ. He is the only one who died to pay for our sins. She insists that her saints represented by the images of people can save her. She has altars in her home and worships all the ones in the Catholic Church. Recently I phoned her. As soon as she answered, she addressed the issue of religion. I witnessed to her about our Lord Jesus Christ. I shared with her my testimonies of the many wonders He has done in my life and my love for Him. She happily shared that she had seen God in a dream. Crying, she told me she saw Jesus crucified at the edge of a large lake. That she saw Him off the cross and she approached Him to make sure He was alive. There were many people who had been rescued from the waters. All the people at the lake shore were about to drown. When she was near to the cross, someone told her to give Jesus a kiss. She was told that He had saved all the people

Divine Revelations through Dreams   109

who were at the lakeshore. I explained to her that God is showing her who is the only one who can save us. I told her that her "saints" are a complete act of disobedience to God's first commandment. We should love God with all our heart and mind. We should not have other Gods and should not make any image or statue of anything to worship it. But the sad thing is she still clings to her belief and follows her religious leaders.

Chapter 14

Walking with God

Most assuredly, I say to you, he who does not enter the sheepfold by the door, but climbs up some other way, the same is a thief and a robber. But he who enters by the door is the shepherd of the sheep. To him the doorkeeper opens, and the sheep hear his voice; and he calls his own sheep by name and leads them out. And when he brings out his own sheep, he goes before them; and the sheep follow him, for they know his voice. Yet they will by no means follow a stranger, but will flee from him, for they do not know the voice of strangers.

John 10:1-5

How do we know whether it is God or is the devil who is speaking to us? There are different signs and they are difficult to understand, because the devil is always trying to confuse us. One of the signs is the fact that God never contradicts His word. He would never tell us to do anything that would cause us to sin. We need to have a close relationship with God in order to recognize His voice. His Word says, *"My sheep hear my voice"* (John 10:27).

112   Breaking Bondages

The following testimony shared by a relative will help us to understand who is speaking to us. She was desperately looking for a document for several days but did not find it. After days of an unfruitful search, she said "God help me find it." Right after she said that, she was able to sense something pointing to the place where the document was. She looked in that place and there it was. The following Biblical quotation will clarify any doubt. *"If I regard iniquity in my heart, The Lord will not hear."* (Psalm 66:18). I asked her two basic questions. Have you accepted that Christ is the only Savior? Have you repented of all your sins and asked God for forgiveness in the name of His Son Jesus Christ? She replied she had not done that yet. Then according to the above scripture it was not God who answered her prayer. God does not respond if we do not ask first for forgiveness. He does not know us personally because we have not given Him the opportunity. The devil can answer to deceive us and make us believe that God is happy with our life style. This person to whom I refer was living in adultery, trapped by some addictions and to sustain her obsession; she had to steal. She thought that her religion would save her, since she attended mass weekly.

We do not know when we will die, but God knows and wants us to be saved. We all are God's creation, but not all are God's children as many people believe. When we believe in Jesus and repent of our sins our citizenship changes. The next scenario would help us understand our status and our rights. We are walking at an unknown place surrounded by unknown people. Suddenly a need arises. We need one hundred dollars or perhaps a camera. We turn around and ask the first person we see for the money or the camera we need. The stranger ignores our request because he/she does not know us. But when a child asks his/her father for the things he/she needs, the father always listens and gives what he/she really needs. God wants to give us what we need but we need to recognize Him as our Lord and Savior. He wants to be our Father.

Good works do not save anyone. To be a good person who never hurts anyone or to go to church often does not bring salvation to our lives. The salvation we have comes through Jesus' sacrifice at Calvary. He came to earth and died for our sins. His wounds healed us through our faith, a sincere repentance of our sins and a desire to obey Him forever. If we could enter to

Walking with God   113

heaven through our works we would be saying that the sacrifice of Jesus on the cross was in vain. He died because through His death He would open the access to paradise again. Jesus overcame death hanging on a wooden cross. Through His death, He pinned the written decree on the cross and ridiculed the devil who believed that he had the victory (Colossians 2:14). I mean by this that the legal demands of the Ten Commandments are valueless when we receive the Grace of God. God's Law was impossible to be obeyed without faith in Jesus Christ. Jesus said: I did not come to remove the Law but to make sure that it is fulfilled (Matt. 5:17)

Unless we are born again, we cannot enter the Kingdom of God (John 3:3). To be born again means a change in our nature that gives us the divine adoption. The Bible says that only those who believe in Jesus Christ have been given the right to become His children, or to be adopted by God (John 1:12). But we all can be His children if we desire it. It is very easy because God does not discriminate against anyone. We just have to present ourselves to Him and tell Him that we recognize His sacrifice on the cross and that we need His forgiveness for all our offenses. Our sincere repenting grants us God's grace and forgiveness. There are only two sides of the coin. If we are not with God, we are with the devil, it's that simple. The apostle Paul said that our struggles are not with flesh and blood but with the powers of the dark world (Ephesians 6:12). The devil is at work twenty four hours a day, seven days of the week to take as many souls as possible to hell. He makes miracles and wonders to deceive people. The devil is always looking for ways to confuse and slyly succeeds. If we analyze what I said earlier we conclude that if it was not God who listened to our request, then is obvious that it was the devil. The same happens when we pray to the statues of saints and miracles are granted. These images cannot remove their own dust and we hope that they can work miracles. The Bible says they have mouths, but cannot speak, have eyes but cannot see and ears but they cannot hear (Psalm 115:5-6). No one who lived and died but Jesus has risen yet, therefore; the dead cannot hear us much less can help in any way (Isaiah 38:18-19).

God taught the apostles how to pray when they asked Him. He taught them the "Lord's Prayer". When we analyze the prayer taught by God, we realize that we have free access to the Father. There is no need of priests as in the days of the Old Testament. Jesus Christ is the high priest that connects us with the Father and intercedes for us. The Lord's Prayer teaches we shall sanctify and praise the name of God before we ask for our needs. He instructed them to seek for the forgiveness of their trespasses in daily basis. Jesus promised whatever we ask in His name will be granted (John 4:13-14). We must be very cautious in the way we pray. There is only one God and we must pray the way He instructed His disciples. When we do not turn to Him through Jesus Christ who is the only mediator, the one who is listening to us and granting our requests is the devil.

God does not always speak loud and clear to us. We could hear Him speaking to us through different manners. He uses His written Word to speak to us most of the time. Many times He uses people such as preachers and prophets. The Holy Spirit speaks through an audible voice in our mind. Sometimes a feeling of peace in our heart or perhaps a dream or a vision gives us the answer to our prayers. How do we know who is talking to us? We just have to ponder about our request and if the answer gives us peace, then we should know that it was God. Remember God gives us peace and the devil takes it away.

God wants to have a close relationship with us. When we are too busy working we do not have time to share with anyone. I had two daily jobs that kept me too tired and busy. One day I asked God if I should keep working the two jobs. Every time I opened the Bible, He showed me the same passage. The passage talks about Martha complaining to Jesus because Mary does not help her to do chores. She leaves everything and sits down to listen to him. Jesus replied to Martha that she was always so worried about unimportant things. He assured Martha that He would never take away what belonged to Mary (Luke 10:38-42). I understood that God was giving the same answer to me. The next day I asked one of my employers for a permit to leave for six months. When six months passed I asked God if I should go back to work and again I had the same response. During that testing time I often received attractive job opportunities. God has slowly taken away from me the love for money and material things and has replaced by a sincere love for Him. I did not return to that job and rejected the other opportunities. Now I have much more time to learn from the Word of God and to serve Him. I have not missed the money earned before and I am much happier. The Lord has given me a peace that is hard to describe; it must be experienced firsthand.

God always hears our prayers but does not always give us the answer we want to hear. It is necessary to give thanks and praise for all He has given us and for all He will give us later. We should not be asking for riches and vane things that could cause our damnation. If we have health, peace and food are more than blessed already. There are many people in the world who have none of these three things. God knows everything we need to fulfill the purpose for which we were brought into this world. It is best to ask for wisdom and discernment for they will prepare us to serve Him. We should also ask for faith and love because through them we can please God and help people in need. I will share the following testimony trying to prevent others from making the same mistakes I've made. I started reading the Bible on my own and that's fine. From the beginning I was guided by the Holy Spirit. He led me through its pages. I had so many questions as it happens to all the new creatures. I sat on my bed to ask Him many questions I had. My heavenly Father sent His Holy Spirit to teach me and every question I have is answered through the Scriptures. I made it a habit of asking for things all day long. I was asking and asking without giving thanks for anything. One day as I opened the Bible, I read a verse that told me that I was like a leech. It was a lesson that convicted me of being disrespectful. I was just asking and asking for things but never thanked God for the favors received (Prov. 30:13-15). I loved the way He corrected me. Since that day I stopped being ungrateful. I learned to give thanks and to praise God for everything.

Chapter 15

Our Best Teacher

For the people shall dwell in Zion at Jerusalem; You shall weep no more. He will be very gracious to you at the sound of your cry; When He hears it, He will answer you. And though the Lord gives you. The bread of adversity and the water of affliction, Yet, your teachers will not be moved into a corner anymore, But your eyes shall see your teachers.

Isaiah 30:19-20

The baptism of the Holy Spirit empowers us to do God's will. The Lord baptized me with His Spirit and with fire. From the beginning of my walk I sensed a need for more of God and was always looking for opportunities to learn. My husband and I went to the beach and there we met a person who claimed to know the Scriptures. I asked him to teach me for I was hungry for the Word. He came once a week and taught me what he knew; I was very happy. I thanked God for putting people in my path to teach me how to know Him better. I also read the Bible on my own with the help of the Holy Spirit. One day I sensed that a particular biblical versus spoke to me in an audible manner. It told me to stay away from liars and deceivers. I did not think He was referring to the person who came to teach me but he stopped coming without any explanation. Every Friday I waited but he never came back. I called and called but he was always too busy to talk to me. I cried because I had no one to teach me and had an insatiable hunger to know more about God. One day right after praying I opened the Bible. Surprisingly I sensed that someone spoke to me again through the Word of God. The voice told me not to cry anymore because from this day the teacher was not going to separate from me. The Lord is amazing. He takes away the people that are going to hurt or confuse us when we trust in Him. Since that day I started to receive so much help. He even gave me a Bible study at home. People gave me so many books that there was not enough time to read them all. No doubt, the Holy Spirit is our best teacher. He teaches and corrects us when we need it. The first thing He does when we invite Him into our heart is to convict us of sin. He needs to live in a clean body and He does everything in order to keep it clean. He makes us feel so bad until we ask God for forgiveness. From the moment we invite Jesus into our hearts, the Holy Spirit does not leave us alone. He is always fighting our daily battles. If you do not believe me, I challenge you to try and see that I do not lie.

The Holy Spirit is the pilot of our life. True Christians not only read the Bible and go to church; they strive to live a Christ-like life full of sacrifices and constant prayer. When we decide to walk with Christ, He gets really happy and takes us by our hand. He treats us as if we were little children. He behaves just like a father or a mother who wants to make sure his/her children are safe. He protects us from the enemy day and night. He teaches us how to defend ourselves against the fiery darts of the evil one (Ephesians 6: 10-20). He gives us power to fight and win any battle against the forces of darkness as we see it in the following quote. *"For the weapons of our warfare are not carnal but are mighty in God for pulling down strongholds"* (2 Corinthians 10:4). This sounds extravagant but it is true.

The enemy continually tempts true Christians. He is upset that they ignore him to dedicate their entire lives to worship God and to take care of His sheep. They live looking for opportunities to serve God because they know that faith without works is worthless (James 2:18). The Lord did not make the trees just to look pretty with their fruits, but He made them for the benefit of His creation. Similarly, we all have a purpose to fulfill. We need to accomplish our purpose or we could be cut off and thrown into the fire as the fig tree that bore no fruit (John 15:6, Luke 3:7-9). To save the sheep from the clutches of the wolf metaphorically speaking, we are dealing directly with the forces of evil. Every time we plant a seed we are tempted in ways that we can only understand when we know the Word of God. The Holy Scriptures recommend that we pray a lot and to be very alert because the enemy is always spying on us (I Pet. 5:8).

The attacks of the enemy increase as we get closer to God. In the beginning I used to be afflicted by the enemy's attack, but know I get comforted because that teaches me that what I am trying is pleasing to God. I endure daily assaults because I am witnessing the works of my Father in heaven. I go to work and there I encounter people trying to make my life difficult. The devil wants to discourage me. He tells me that no matter what I do, I will never be right with God. I go home and I find my kids arguing and fighting with each other. My children tell me that I am the worst of mothers. My brothers tell me that I am mentally unstable because I read the scriptures. The people at church persecute me for telling the truth. When I see these problems, I immediately realize that they are bouts and praying is the solution. Our battles are won on our knees. I tell my Father in heaven that I am confident that He will fight my battles and He quickly comes to my aid. The beauty of this is that the devil begins these problems trying to turn us away from God, but my heavenly Father changes evil for good. While the devil is attacking me, I pray in front of whoever is present. Faithless people end up believing in Jesus.

I read about a true story of a missionary. He came to evangelize cannibals where many believed in Jesus including the leader of the tribe. Years later an incredulous scientist came to that same island. He saw people reading the Scriptures and took them as ignorant. The chief of the tribe came to him and said in a low voice. I know you do not believe in the Bible but you should at least thank God that we do believe. If we did not believe in Jesus Christ and His word you would now be boiling in a pot to feed as dinner to my tribe. What a strong message!

God opens doors unexpectedly. My husband and I went to drop off our daughter at a birthday party for one of her friends. I stayed in the car waiting for my husband. God wanted me to witness to the father of my daughter's friend. He asked my husband for me and when he learned that I was in the car, he came to greet me. He gave me a sincere hug without knowing me. I felt that he needed God desperately due to his divorce in progress. I invited him to meet him. He was eager to talk about his financial problems and impending divorce. I took the opportunity God gave me. I told him Jesus Christ is the only one able to help us solve our problems. I invited him to trust in God at all times since He promised to fight our battles. The testimonies of people bring hope to our lives when we see that there is no way out. The faith of others is contagious and transforms our mind. He invited us to his house because he wanted to know more about God. I thank God for His Holy Spirit that teaches us His Word and helps us to use it for the benefit of others.

Chapter 16

Doubts and Miracles

When God wants to bring us closer to Him, He intensifies our trials. My mother died four months after my brother had been kidnapped. I found out that she was very ill because she told me that she could not sleep nor eat because of a stomachache. My family in Mexico was not giving her the right attention she needed. She wanted me to ask my brothers to take her to the hospital. They would not listen to me either because I left the Catholic Church. I called my brother who lived in the Bahamas so that he could ask my brothers in Mexico. That same night my mother was transported to the hospital where she was immediately supplied with blood. Her red blood cells were too low. The next day I learned by divine revelation that God was going to take her soon. I had prayed for God to give me the opportunity to take care of my mother the same way she did for her mother. I left for Mexico the next day and I found her trying to eat some soup. She was very surprised to see me there. Every time I called her I tried to encourage her to fight for her life through the faith in Jesus Christ. My dad told her that I was there to bring her relief because he too believed in my faith. I replied that I was not capable of bringing relief to anyone. The Lord has given us the power to heal people in Jesus's name. I probably made an error in not meditating my answer at that moment. Now I know that miracles occur because of our faith but then I was afraid of offending God our Lord. God gives us gifts and power to make miracles happen in His name. We must just ask with immense faith in the name of our Lord Jesus

122   Breaking Bondages

Christ. At that time I did not know because I had not read enough of the Holy Scriptures and because I was barely learning.

The Lord reveals His plans to His children (Amos 3:7). Before leaving for Mexico to be with my mother in her last days, my family and I had dinner at a restaurant. While we were waiting for our dinner a man who passed right in front of us had a written biblical phrase on his shirt. The phrase captured my daughter's attention and she asked me to read it as well. It said: *"by his wounds we are healed"* (Isaiah 53:5 NIV). The phrase increased my faith that my mother could live longer. It was the same phrase my brother recited before dying. That phrase was a revelation given to the prophet Isaiah where he was shown the mystery of salvation through the death of our Lord Jesus Christ. When I saw my mom, I shared with her the message on the shirt. It immediately brought her hope. What I did not know was that the healing spoken in the message is about the spirit. For our Father in heaven healing the spirit is more important than healing the body. What He was sharing with me was that He was going to heal my mom's spirit. We must make sure that our spirit endures for eternity. Our Father in heaven will equip us with a new body if we are capable of maintaining our spirit alive. We come into this world with a purpose in which our Father sent us. Once that purpose is completed he takes us with him. If we do not accomplish our purpose, He cuts us from the face of earth. We are thrown into a fire so that we burn because we were trees that did not produce fruit (John 15:6).

God sent me to Mexico just in time to share the Gospel with my mom. My dear mother had only four conscious days for me to be able to speak with her. From the day I arrived I devoted my time to take care for her and to try to make sure that she would spend the eternity in heaven. First thing I did was to pray God in the name of our Lord Jesus Christ to take her pain away. After praying, my mother finally went to sleep for the first time in days. She was so tired that no noise woke her from her sleep. The excruciating pain she had kept her awake day and night. I also rebuked all kinds of evil spirits that roamed around my mother in the name of my Lord Jesus Christ. The next day I kept praying and reading the Scriptures to her. My mother fell asleep while I was reading to her so I decided to let her rest. As I passed by the open window opposite to her bed, to put the Bible on a shelf, something

Doubts and Miracles   123

particularly strange happened to me. I felt a strong tug on the left side of my chest and heard a static noise in the blouse I was wearing. It was very painful; I felt as if someone had wanted to pull out my heart.

Our ignorance makes us make mistakes. In the scriptures we read: "*Or how can one enter a strong man's house and plunder his goods, unless he first binds the strong man?*" (Matthew 12:29). Religion and vices are evil spirits that take over the minds of the people and become the owners of those houses. The people who live there do not feel them. The demons are so sure of having them under their control that they do not bother them. When the demons feel threatened by a person who has given his/her heart to the Lord, they start fighting. The beauty of this is that they cannot do anything without God's permission. The Holy Spirit protects us as Jesus said it would be. It did not occur to me that I had been attacked by one of the demons casted out when I prayed for my mom. They tried to kill me by removing my heart. I think my Lord Jesus Christ did not want me to be frightened. Meanwhile in Los Angeles my family had a very difficult time. The devil tried to do everything possible for me to come back and leave things as they were in Mexico. My husband called me very upset for he did not want to deal with the problem my oldest daughter was causing. My youngest daughter just thirteen years old told me not to return until I had fulfilled my mission there. God used her to comfort me.

The mission was accomplished in ten days. My heavenly Father sent me to Mexico with a purpose that was very difficult to fulfill. The opposition was great because the devil did not want to lose a soul that was approaching the end. God took me over with the message of salvation for my mother. At the same time He was giving me the opportunity to take care of her when she needed it. Since my mom got sick I prayed for her salvation because in order to be saved we must be born again. Catholics do not know that because they rarely read the Bible. When they read it, they do not understand it due to lack of spiritual discernment. One of the first things I did when I got there was to advise her to repent of all her sins. I begged the Lord to forgive her. Four days after my arrival to Mexico my mom stopped talking and just slept a lot. One day she drowsily opened her eyes and smiled when she saw me sitting next to her bed. At that time I took the opportunity to ask her if she believed that Jesus Christ was her only savior. Her response was quick and she said "oh yes". The next day before dawn I stood beside her. I put my hand on her stomach and prayed God for healing. I saw instead of my hand a white hand landing on my mom's stomach. Along with the hand shined a small light that brought me hope. I felt something very special at that time. I shared the vision with my sister and my dad. I told them to have faith that a miracle would happen. My dad replied with a question. Are you sure you are not crazy? I felt sorrow and anger for his lack of faith. Miracles happen for people to believe and thus increase their faith. From that day on my mom got worse and did not speak coherently again. We would sit her up to feed her with liquefied food that I prepared with meat broths and vegetables. I made sure she ate well and drank enough water. In the same week we took her to the doctor. He told us that he could not try more chemotherapy because she was very weak and could not handle it. We opted to take her home where she had said she wanted to die.

Transporting her to her home was a disaster. It seemed that by moving her we would hurt her stomach. It was worse once we arrived home. She writhed screaming in pain and we could not do anything to help. That night my brother went back to the city to ask the doctor for a stronger pain killer. The doctor prescribed morphine and another medicine to relieve pain. Her suffering pushed one brother to ask God to take her already. With pain he told her how much we loved her, but that it was better if she went to rest. As if her life or death depended on her. That night as she writhed in pain they prayed a rosary by her bed. That prayer refreshed in her memory that whole litany of which she so accustomed. She was the praying person in town for all occasions. All night in desperation she recited the Hail Mary like a broken record. The Bible says that those repetitions instead of pleasing God offend Him (Matthew 6:5). I would tell her to talk to Jesus because He is the Savior. She could not hear me and just kept endlessly repeating her "Hail Mary". The day I arrived in Mexico she told me that she had not prayed the rosary because she could not. To hear that made me happy. I prayed every day that my heavenly Father would cover her with the blood of our Lord Jesus Christ. He did it and she was not allowed to go further offending God. God warns us against using vane repetitions when we pray for they come not from the

Doubts and Miracles   125

heart but of the mind. The mind is easily manipulated by the enemy that makes us believe the religions which have been created by him.

We did everything that was in our power to help my mother. The early days of her agony we injected morphine and other drugs and so she rested a little. Days later nothing took away her pain. The friends of her along with my sister and her sisters were there praying rosaries. She did not receive any benefit from their prayers because the pain would not stop. While they recited their prayers I would ask God to forgive them for they knew not that they offended Him. They asked the images and statues of people to intercede for her before God. They lit candles to images placed in altars around the house. The Bible clearly says that the only intercessor before our heavenly Father is Jesus Christ (1Tim. 2:5). After they finished their litanies I would stand beside her to pray. I would ask someone to accompany me, and we prayed the way our Lord Jesus Christ recommended to the apostles. *"Again I say to you that if two of you agree on earth concerning anything that they ask, it will be done for them by My Father in heaven"* (Matthew 18:19). I recognized to God with all my heart that only He could deliver my mom from that great suffering, the terrible pain caused by cancer of the stomach. I reminded God about His promises and that I believed them. God quickly came to her help and took away the pain every time I asked. She would sleep for up to three hours straight. I was able to rest too. When the pain returned people would look for me. Several people noticed that only my prayers took away my mom's pain. Despite not accepting my spirituality, at that time they were able to see that my prayers were effective unlike theirs.

Chapter 17

We are in bondage with the world

And a servant of the Lord must not quarrel but be gentle to all, able to teach, patient, in humility correcting those who are in opposition, if God perhaps will grant them repentance, so that they may know the truth, and that they may come to their senses and escape the snare of the devil, having been taken captive by him to do his will.

2 Timothy 2:24-26

Disobedience to God produces bondage, but the Holy Spirit gives us power to break them. The following testimony reveals a great truth. During her last week my mom would just call my name. Seven of her children were present along with her husband. It seemed as if I had been her only child. She called me every time she needed something. She even would call my name to her other daughters. She spoke incoherently saying things difficult to understand for people who do not know God. She would say to me "Maria loosen the rope" and "open the door" in a desperate tone. Two days before she died while we were bathing her, she seemed distracted and annoyed. It seemed like something was happening at the time that was torturing her terribly. She desperately said wash me in cold water. My mother feared God and cared very much for salvation. She always reminded us that we had a soul to save. She lived a life of sacrifice, weekly fasting trying to earn her salvation. She never had any fun, was very devoted to her religion. She spent hours praying in church every day. While she was able to, there was not a day where she would not pray rosaries and novenas. She believed that the Rosary was the first step to heaven and for that reason she would recite them over and over assuring her entrance. My poor mom was so deceived by that demon of Catholicism. But the Holy Spirit searches our hearts, knows our intentions and breaks our chains. God sent me to cut her bonds pursuant to His promises made to all who love Him. That was the reason why God allowed her to look at me as her only way out. I was her only child who had accepted Jesus as Lord and Savior. Her other children were more interested in their religion than in salvation. I was seen as a stranger to them and mentally unbalanced. It is written that people who do not know God would view us this way. "For those who live according to the flesh set their minds on the things of the flesh, but those *who live* according to the Spirit, the things of the Spirit" (Romans 8:5). I had peace regardless of their disapproval because my Lord Jesus Christ was very close to me all the time I was in Mexico taking care of my mom.

Why did her mom ask María to loosen her lash was a question asked by all who listened to her. Besides releasing the lash my mom also asked me to open the door. I had the same question. Her last night with us she suffered horribly. I begged for one hour or so to my Heavenly Father to alleviate her suffering and He did it for a while. My heavenly Father took pity and let her rest for an hour after much prayer and pleading on my part. It was past midnight, when wearied and sad I went to my room to continue talking to God. I implored God to forgive my mother. I reminded Him of another of His promises that assured me I could trust my Father in heaven. Guided by the Holy Spirit I randomly opened the Bible and I received a big surprise. The book was showing me why my mom had asked me to untie the rope that was binding her. It talks about the power given to the disciples of Jesus to free or to bind people. "Assuredly, I say to you, whatever you bind on earth will be bound in heaven, and whatever you loose on earth will be loosed in heaven" (Matthew 18:18). Disciples are those who follow God's commandments and their only God is our Lord Jesus Christ. I pondered that for a moment and then I realized I was a disciple of Jesus. I had just recently decided to give my life to Christ my savior and desired to follow Him always. As I read the phrase, I immediately understood that God was telling me to unfasten my mom's bandage. Led by the Holy Spirit I began to pray, "Mom in the name of my Lord Jesus Christ I release all ties and stronghold so you can go to rest in the presence of God forever." She died three hours later on November seventh. Seven is the number of perfection which means that something is accomplished according to God's perfect will. For me that meant that the purpose of my trip was fulfilled. I freed my mom from the trap of the devil and she was left to rest forever.

When we read the Holy Scriptures, we learn that we have ties that come from our ancestors for generations. We realize that we are under the snare of the devil who keeps us captive to do his will. When we disobey God's commandments, we are chaining ourselves and our children up to the third and fourth generation (Exodus 20:2-5). We must live in obedience to break those bonds in the name of Jesus Christ. My mom's idolatry and disobedience to God along with all the idolatry of her ancestors who held the same religion was keeping her in bondage to the devil. God revealed my mother's salvation through a dream. A few days after her death, I dreamt that I picked her up from her deathbed. I took her in my arms and walked with her through a small door. We barely fit in that door. The Bible says the door to heaven is very narrow (Luke 13:24). He clearly showed me that my mom was saved. He does not fail to fulfill His promises because of His great love and mercy. My mom's greatest desire was salvation but never learned how to achieve it. She was a victim of a religion that does not focus on teaching the truth, but rather uphold religious traditions. I think that she could not die because my heavenly Father knew how affected I would be if my mom did not go to heaven. I pleaded with Him not to take her unless she was saved and I am sure He heard my cry because He is my Father. "Or

130   Breaking Bondages

what man is there among you who, if his son asks for bread, will give him a stone? Or if he asks for a fish, will he give him a serpent? If you then, being evil, know how to give good gifts to your children, how much more will your Father who is in heaven give good things to those who ask Him!" (Matthew 7:9-11). It seems to me that the Lord allowed my mom to see the two places where people go after death. She wanted to enter the gate of heaven but could not go because the door was closed and she was not free. She saw that I had both, the key to open the door and the tools to break her chains. Glory be to God!

In the Bible we read that when people die their spirits go to two different places. One place is Hades and the other is paradise or Abraham's bosom. This conclusion is drawn from the passage of the rich man and Lazarus the beggar (Luke 16:19-31). One is a place where there is no suffering and the other one there is horrifying torture. According to this revelation in that place the heat is agonizing and people are regretful and desperate. The Lord has shown me this place through a dream. The place was extremely hot and dry, people walking in hot ashes. The rich man was in the hot place I saw in my dream. From where he was, he beheld Lazarus very calm in a place where he did not suffer anything. Desperate the rich man asked Abraham to allow Lazarus to wet a finger and put it on his tongue to soothe the terrible thirst. He also asked Abraham to send Lazarus to earth to warn his brothers and family about his suffering so they do not suffer the same fate. But Abraham's answer was completely disappointing. He informed the rich man that people would not believe anything Lazarus would say because God has commanded Moses and the prophets and people do not believe. Besides that Abraham also explained to him that it was not possible to leave from any of the two places because there was a great abyss between them. God teaches us everything we need to know. To convince me even further my mom was saved He showed me through another dream days after her departure. I did not know anything about Abraham's bosom, but in a dream I saw two people walking on the other side of a river dressed with long robes. I saw them walking away from me but I knew that one was my mom and the other person was Abraham. My heavenly Father has taught me many mysteries and that makes me love Him more each day.

My mom was allowed to see the place of torment. This conclusion explains why she asked me in desperation to bathe her in cold water. God was showing her where she might have gone because of her idolatry and lack of seeking the truth which is discussed throughout the Scriptures. Nevertheless, the Lord made a promise to His children. Their house and family would be saved. He has disclosed to me the fulfillment of His promise by granting my mom the opportunity to see her chains. He showed her the problem and the provision. God is faithful and righteous in every sense of the word. Something totally weird happened during her funeral. No priest was available to say the customary funeral Mass before taking the body to the cemetery. A priest came to celebrate a mass the day my mother died. The casket almost fell to the ground in the very entrance of the chapel. The protective glass was broken. It seems as if she was trying to say that she did not want anything from that religion. At least that is what I understood.

Chapter 18

Religion and Salvation: Two Different Things

Pure and undefiled religion before God and the Father is this: to visit orphans and widows in their trouble, and to keep oneself unspotted from the world.

James 1:27

I read in a book of Spanish literature an appealing phrase that says: "religion is the opium of people." In this story written by Miguel de Unamuno a priest suffered by teaching a doctrine which he does not believe in. He does it only to earn the support of his family and to keep people busy believing something. He really was a lying atheist who sincerely cares for people. Opium is one of many drugs that numb the senses and removes the ability to make right decisions. What a great truth this is in terms of religion. Many doctrines that are not completely based on the Bible and the grace of God to reach salvation are far from the truth. Each religion makes people

134   Breaking Bondages

believe that they have the truth. They claim only through these religions they will be saved and instruct their followers to not accept anyone who are not of the same religion. Over the centuries, Jews have been humiliated and despised around the world. The devil hates them because salvation came from them and he makes their life difficult. The Word of God says those who bless them be blessed and those who curse them be cursed. They were the chosen people where our Savior came from.

Some religions lead us to worship images and statues of stone or wood and organize celebrations in honor of those idols. The statues are carried in procession through the streets where people sing hymns to them. These idols are worshipped as if they were God and then people deny that they adore them. They argue that they only venerate them. Adoration and veneration means the same when it refers to worship. It is giving the honor to a person but such honor only belongs to the Lord. Such an action is total disobedience to the first commandment of God about not honoring images or statues (Exodus 20:5). People in their ignorance greatly offend our Lord Jesus Christ. This same religion denies the truth about Jesus Christ as our only Savior and presents others as mediators. The Holy Scriptures clearly state Jesus Christ is the only mediator between us and the Father (1 Tim.2: 5). We do not need to ask any saint, apostle or Virgin to intercede for us. The godly people of the past should be used only as an example to live our lives the way they did, but we should not see them as idols. They also make people believe that salvation is earned by works. Their doctrine invents pagan rituals as penance for the forgiveness of their sins. People walk on their knees for long distances to visit religious images in gratitude for helping with their afflictions. What they do not know is the devil is behind those miraculous signs. As I explained it before the images are disobedience to God. How can people expect that it is God who is responding to the petitions made to idols? (2 Corinthians 11:14).

Salvation comes by the grace of God derived from our faith in Christ Jesus. A well-known religion leads people to believe that they are able to forgive sins and that is obviously not true. God is the only one who can forgive sins. They call their religious leader father ignoring the Word of God that warns us against that. *"Do not call anyone on earth your father; for One is your*

Religion and Salvation: Two Different Things   135

Father, He who is in heaven." (Matthew 23:9). Other doctrines teach that people reincarnate into animals and they worship them. Other religions deceive their followers and induce them to sacrifice their lives and those of others. They promise many attractive rewards in eternity. Such is the case of the Islam. They promise if they kill Jewish people, they would receive many maidens for wives in heaven. In the religion I used to practice people were offended when someone uttered the name of Jehovah which means "the unchanging, eternal, self-existent God," the "I am that I am,"(Exodus 3:14). The Israelites made this name in a way that people could not pronounce it because of its Holiness and they were not worth it. They put various consonants together without vowels impossible to utter. The Lord did not give them a name, He only told them that He was the one Who is, the one Who Was and the one Who Will be for the eternity. Later on people added points as in the Hebrew language, they have sounds of vowels and they are now translated to all the languages. Others definitely deny that Jesus is God. They contend that He is only the son of God, a created being, and the brother of the archangel Michael and of Lucifer.

Salvation is free and easy to reach, believe it or not. We do not need a religion to achieve it; all we need is a close relationship with God. We just simply need to confess that Jesus Christ came to earth to die for our salvation and that He is our only Lord and Savior. Salvation cannot be earned through work or praying rosaries, novenas or anything like that. It is a free gift from God that we did not deserve. We could make thousands of sacrifices but if Jesus did not die to redeem us, the gate to heaven would have remained closed. Jesus came to earth to destroy the works of the devil who believed that death would last for eternity. Jesus conquered death by hanging on a cross and opening paradise's door. But this does not mean that the gate of hell is now closed. Now we have two options to choose from. We either follow Jesus or go to hell. If we follow Jesus we must first repent of all our sins and ask God to forgive them. We must love God with all our heart, our soul and our being and obey Him in all that He commands according to the sacred Scriptures.

We do not need to follow a doctrine of men. In fact the Bible warns against trusting Men instead of God (Jeremiah 17:5). When I witness to peo-

136 Breaking Bondages

ple, they usually ask me which church I belong to. What is my religion? If I say I am a Christian they ask to which denomination I belong. Many times people have told me I need to be under a denomination to have support whenever I have problems. I answer them that my protection comes from above. The only thing we need is to have a close relationship with God. When we receive Jesus as our Lord and Savior, the heavenly Father sends us His Spirit to protect us every day. Jesus said that to enter the Kingdom of God we must be born again of water and the Spirit (John 3:5). Before receiving the Spirit of God through His Son Jesus Christ our spirit was dead. When our spirit revives we are no longer the same. We are new creatures guided by the Holy Spirit who has transformed us. All the old things have passed; God has made **everything** new in our lives. The Spirit of God leads us on the path of truth and we are alerted before committing a grave sin. We still sin but not as much as we did before because the Holy Spirit guards us. The genes of the devil in our flesh we bring from the sin of Adam in the garden are against our spirit. If we keep in constant prayer and thanksgiving for all the blessings we receive daily, the Holy Spirit protects us against the temptations. We no longer need to go to any advocate to speak for us. The Holy Spirit who lives in us communicates directly with our heavenly Father and presents to God our needs.

In the Old Testament we read God appointed a High Priest who served as mediator. Jesus came to teach us how to obey God's commandments. After His death and resurrection He sent us the Holy Spirit to warn and protect us against offending the Lord. When we fall into temptation, Jesus, our High Priest mediates on our behalf to the Father for our forgiveness. The curtain of the temple was torn from top to bottom at the moment when Jesus died to give us free access to the Father. The beauty of this is that we do not need to wait until we die to find out if we are saved. We can live confidently because we know that when we leave this world, we are moving to a much better one. Salvation is attained here on earth by grace through faith in Jesus Christ. This is where we secure the pass to enter heaven. Once we have that, we can hardly lose it because the Lord does everything possible to keep us saved unless we so wish to stay away from Him. The Bible warns us about turning away from God. We must take good care of the great salvation granted when we believed that Jesus is our only Savior. The body, which is the temple of the Holy Spirit must be kept clean. No one seems to know what the blasphemy of the Holy Spirit is, but the Bible says that it is the only unforgivable sin. For me blaspheming the Holy Spirit means to do what God does not like after knowing it is wrong. We quench the Spirit over and over disregarding all the warnings. I understand that the only people who can blaspheme the Holy Spirit are the ones who had received it. When people sin without the Holy Spirit, they really do not know what they are doing. Jesus asked His father to forgive the people who crucified Him for they did not know better (Luke 23:34). The ones who persevere to the end shall be saved.

The ten commandments of God could not be met without the sacrifice of Jesus on Calvary. They were not given to save anyone but to teach the difference between good and evil. Therefore we say salvation cannot be earned with deeds. Jesus said He came not to abolish the law but to fulfill it (Matthew 5:17-18). The Bible says that all have sinned and we were all short of the glory of God. Jesus came to justify us freely by His grace and forgiveness (Rom. 3:23-24). God would like us to obey the commandments but He knows our weaknesses, therefore He only asks us to have faith and follow him. You may think that this is hard to do but I tell you it is not. Life with God is much easier to carry because He guides us step by step. When God fills your heart, you do not need the worldly things once enjoyed. The children of God do not belong to this world even if they live in the world. When we are born again our mind changes and we become a new person. We do not think about ourselves only, but we love and serve God as well as our neighbor. We are committed to find ways to please God. We just want to fulfill the purpose that God has for us from the moment He adopted us as His children. We want to bear abundant fruit to avoid being cut off from the ground and thrown into the fire to burn. Obviously the people who hurt others and who seek only their convenience do not fear God. In other words they are not born again and therefore will not see the kingdom of God (John 3:3).

Chapter 19

From Darkness to Light

*But as many as received Him, to them He gave the right to
become children of God, to those who believe in His name:*

John 1:12

We are all God's creation, but only those who believe in Him are
adopted as His children. When people do not have a relationship
with God, they see things that do not seem ordinary but they do not give
them importance. Without God, our spirit is dead and we cannot have direct
communication with our Lord. Now that I know Him, I have come to the
conclusion that He was always watching me but I did not see Him because
I was living in darkness. We are spiritually dead because we inherited the
sin of Adam and Eve. Their disobedience alienated them from the Spirit of
God that gives eternal life. Death did not exist while they were in the garden.
Sin entered through the stomach and its consequence is death. By eating
the forbidden fruit Adam and Eve were bringing the genes of Satan to the
body. The following verse supports the point. "The heart *is* deceitful above
all *things*, and desperately wicked; Who can know it?" (Jeremiah 17:9).

The dominium of the Garden of Eden God gave to men was transferred
to Satan. From the moment Adam and Eve sinned, they lost all control and

were thrown out of the garden. Now we all are born with a depraved nature and the fleshly desires rule our daily lives. We now have a sinful nature that lust for the things of the world instead of the spiritual things. Our body is our enemy since it drags us to do all the things that lead to eternal death. This explains why there is so much crime and evil in the world. That is why we sin every day even unintentionally. The worst of all this is that we are not aware of the trap where we are kept in. If we are not aware, much less can we try to come out of it? We need the grace of our Lord Jesus Christ that comes by faith. Faith comes from listening to the Word of God through someone sent to us (Romans 10:14-15).

How can we revive the spirit of life? When the Lord sends us His grace, we need to make the right choice. God has given us the free will. When God sends someone to give us the message of salvation through Jesus' death and resurrection, He is showing mercy for us. We can choose between believe or not to believe the message. If we believe the gospel of Jesus, we will receive faith, and our faith will activate the grace of God. His grace will grant us forgiveness. The forgiveness of God breaks our chains and revives our spirit that had otherwise been dead. If we decide to follow God we will have eternal life. The Apostle Paul explains the two bases for salvation. He says that you must confess with your mouth that Jesus is Lord and believe in your heart that God raised him from the dead in order to be saved. Once we have decided to follow the recommendations made above, we will receive the promise Jesus made before ascending to heaven. He told His disciples that He would leave but would not leave them alone. He promised them a counselor, which is the Holy Spirit who proceeds from the Father. He assured us anything we ask the Father in the name of His Son Jesus Christ will be granted. When people receive the Holy Spirit their lives are transformed, their lives become totally different. The fruits of the Spirit begin to manifest through their actions. People can notice changes in their behavior such as love, joy, peace, longsuffering, kindness, goodness, faithfulness, gentleness, self control (Galatians 5:22-23). They try to understand why those radical changes are happening, but cannot.

A problem arises from the day we receive the Holy Spirit. A powerful enemy starts to harass us, but we do not need to worry. The Spirit of God which lives in us is much more powerful than the devil and with Him we will always overcome every temptation. People who have the Spirit of God will not hurt anyone. They have love for all as Jesus Christ loved us and gave His life for our salvation. People who have Christ in their heart always think about others and how to please God. Jesus said true Christians would be known by their fruits (Matthew 7:20).

Recognizing the divine protection

The Lord has a plan for each of His children and it is manifested through our daily lives. God has been molding my character through a life marked by pain and hardships. My life has been in danger many times but I have not gone yet for the Lord has protected me. Hunger forced me along with my brothers and sisters to look for the daily food dodging all kinds of dangers, which were doubled just because I am a girl. Living in my village was difficult because poisonous animals and wild beasts surrounded us. In order to survive it was necessary to work in dangerous places. It was common to walk among snakes and scorpions to get our daily bread. The food was very scarce. Even the most basic needs such as clothing and shoes were difficult to meet. I grew up in an area infested with mosquitoes ravaging our bodies with all kinds of diseases. I grew up with the body covered with sores and scars left by the sufferings endured. Poverty, humiliation, rape and needs of every sort awakened in me the desire to achieve all that I needed in my childhood and youth. Now I know that the devil tried to end my life but could not do so because God always protected me.

My hardships increased when I started Middle School. Now I had to get up earlier in order to help my mother with chores and catch the only bus to take us to school. It was a two hour ride each way daily. My father immigrated to the United States every year in search of work but never found good opportunities. He left us alone with my mom who scarcely provided us with food while doing laundry in a river. The Middle School at that time was morning and evening, so we left home at six a.m. to return around seven

142   Breaking Bondages

p.m. My mother struggled just to give five pesos a day to each of us. We were four siblings attending school at the time. The bus fare cost us four pesos, which left us with one peso to buy food. Two potatoes or cold bean tacos sold by a girl was the only thing we could afford. My mom prepared homemade tortillas with salt to feed us before we left to school. We raised a few chickens, and sold their eggs to raise money for school. We had milk and cheese only during the summer because it was the only time we had enough food for the cows. We had a few cows but we did not have a pasture for them. They were fed with what they found along the roadside. With much sacrifice by both of my parents I completed Middle School.

The dangers were defied every day. In various occasions I escaped dying from venomous animals, assaults and accidents such as drowning and trees falling. When I was fourteen years old my parents moved to a solitary place to sell food to the workers of a road under construction. My mother was expecting my two younger twin siblings. We lived in a cardboard and straw hut without any security. My Dad again left us alone disregarding my mom's condition and immigrated to the United States as he did every year. My mother lived in fear for me. It was very common for girls of my age to be abducted and raped. Thank God no such thing happened there. The road workers were certainly people sent by God to protect us. One day some criminals who wanted to assault the payroll truck took my mom and me under hostage when the police chased them. They were two men who used to eat in our dining hut. They bore high-caliber weapons and seemed to be intoxicated. They knew that they would be safe as long as they were next to us. They were right, God was protecting us. The police waited close by hiding in a curve until the thieves went out. They threatened to kill us if we had said anything. When the thieves left us they were captured. My mother could barely move due to her thirteenth pregnancy. She was in the seventh month of pregnancy with twins, very poorly nourished without any extra care or vitamins. She gave birth to my twin brother and sister on her forty-fourth birthday.

When I moved to the city to attend High School I thought that my life was going to be better but it got worse. When my twin brother and sister were born we returned to my hometown. I started working in a restaurant where I met a gentleman and his daughter who offered me the opportunity to continue studying. That was my greatest desire. They offered me food and shelter in exchange for cleaning their house in the city. But I was cheated, because when I got to that house they just wanted me to work without giving me time to go to school. I enrolled myself in the school disregarding their insults for my delays. I got lost a few times on my way to school; I did not know anyone to help me in the city nor did I know the bus routes. On Friday of my first week at school I was told that I could not stay in their house. I went home for the weekend but wanted to continue studying. On Monday I returned to school without having a place to spend the night. During the day I talked to some classmates about my situation. A girl named Laura offered to help me. She took me to the house of some people she knew and asked if I could stay with them for a while. A very poor family opened their door to me gladly. I stayed with that family during my first year of high school but I moved because I was sexually harassed by one of their boys.

After I left that house, I lived in many others. Problems arose everywhere I went. There is a saying pertaining to my situation, "The dead and squatter stink after 3 days". I was often humiliated for being poor. I went to school morning and afternoon trying to use the time wisely. In the morning I attended a secretarial school and went to the High School in the afternoon. With my secretarial diploma I worked in a few offices where I only lasted a short time. There was always envy and jealousy. I lost in every situation for I was poor and did not have influential relatives to advocate for me. Working hard and going from one place to another I was able to earn a BA degree in business administration. My miseries increased when I tried to get a job in my field. The lack of influential relatives and friends was a problem that always haunted me. Everywhere I applied they wanted to take advantage of my youth and my poverty. The solutions to my problems were still far away since I was walking in darkness without God. God was giving me the bread of adversity and the water of affliction to get my attention but my heart was way too hard to notice it.

The hardships kept increasing steadily. I was forced to move to the United States because of my pregnancy as a result of a rape. When I found out that I was pregnant I was devastated for I did not know what to do. I was terrified and did not know how to tell my parents. My father always threatened us with the worst if we did that. He told my sisters and I that we should forget we had parents. I was so desperate that I tried to look for the rapist to move with him but my fate was different. God used that person to carry out his plan in my life and I have forgiven him. The Lord sent a person to convince me of moving far away. To get my mother's permission I had to confess the truth to her. She sadly said that it was best for me to move in order to avoid being humiliated and despised by my relatives and friends. She gave me all her savings to pay for my bus trip to Tijuana where I had to wait for the opportunity to cross the border. I was raped when I accepted a ride from an acquaintance who offered to take me to a place near by where I worked helping my sister. Instead of taking me to my destination, he took me to a faraway orchard where he abused me. I managed to run away from this man who intended to keep me as his concubine.

My life in Los Angeles went from bad to worse. Pushed by the need of a home for my baby, I was forced to accept a wrong relationship. I moved to live with a person who suffered from a great emotional trauma and certain addictions. My situation worsened because I suddenly found myself living with a stranger who had three children. I needed a home and he needed a babysitter for his children who were abandoned by a drug-addicted mother. He was an emotionally disturbed man and I was forbidden to know the home phone number. He wanted to make sure that I did not talk to anyone. I was enclosed in four walls where I could not open the curtains. I felt so lonely in an unknown world, expecting an unwanted child and surrounded by strangers. When my daughter was three months old I escaped from this situation that further worsened my life. I went from house to house suffering humiliation even though I paid rent. I was forced to leave because my daughter used to cry a lot and that disturbed them. People say that when expecting mothers cry a lot their children are born likewise. My daughter and I had to live most of the time in public parks so we did not annoy the people where we rented a room. In the parks I was haunted by evil people seeking to take advantage of my situation. I dare to say that God made me invisible on several occasions to protect us from imminent danger. On more than one occasion I saw strangers who wanted to assault me reacted strangely. I have no words to thank God for all He has done for me.

God is our refuge in tribulation

For He has not despised nor abhorred the affliction of the afflicted;
Nor has He hidden His face from Him; but when He cried to Him, He heard.

Psalm 22:24

God created human beings in His image with feelings and thoughts; he did not create us to be robots. Robots do not think or feel anything. They do not have a soul that needs to be saved. In order to save our souls, human beings need to suffer. The reward for suffering is the eternal companionship of God. He is with us to comfort us, strengthen us and give us of his Spirit. Pain is one of the tools God uses to make us grow in faith and in spiritual maturity. The pain drives us to overcome our fears and repairs our souls. Pain is an open window to look beyond our means. It is a line that has as purpose to connect us with God. The following Bible verse shows us God's promises for all who seek Him. "The Lord will strengthen him on his bed of illness; You will sustain him on his sickbed" (Psalm 41:3).

We are born with a depraved nature that blinds us from understanding our horrible fate. We live in the world offending our Creator every day without any regrets. I too was deceived by a religion that taught idolatry and disobedience to God. I disregarded the commandment of God to love Him above ALL! I instead danced and sang praises to the images and statues of women and men settled in the temples. I had mentioned earlier that God walked with me and protected me many times but I never thanked Him. I instead kept offending Him by showing my gratitude to what I believed were my intercessors. I naively practiced witchcraft and fasted for the devil. I did not eat meat for nine days and at midnight had to say a prayer to the soul of the derailed soldier. The name caught my attention but I was told that he was a saint that will grant me what I needed. I believed and proceeded with the hex. At midnight for nine days I burned a piece of cardboard with the name of the person I wished to affect. First I put some special oil in my mouth, and then I sprayed it on the paper. After pronouncing the name of the person a number of times, I set it on fire. How ignorant I was to offend my heavenly

Father that way. I behaved so wrong and I deserved all my sufferings and much more. When we do not know God, we walk in darkness stumbling and falling down. He sees us from far away and feels sorry. When we have fallen to the bottom of the abyss and we are drowning, He approaches with open arms to rescue us. In our desperation we acknowledge His existence and ask for help. My Holy Father showed me how great His love is. He had compassion for me and pulled me out from the frivolous life I was living. I should rather say that He rescued me from a muddy tarn where I did not have a way out.

God hears the prayers of the righteous

"Call to Me, and I will answer you, and show you great and mighty things, which you do not know."

Jeremiah 33:3

I met a Christian person who witnessed to me about God and recommended that I read the Bible. People seek God only when they need Him, and at the time I needed Him very much. When I was alone with my daughter without a place to live I realized that only God could help me. With my low salary I could only pay for a little room for my daughter and me. So I decided to seek God. I started to read the Scriptures and ask Him for help. He heard my prayers and soon I had a better job. God represented me in the interview that was in English. I spoke very little English, but with God's help I answered their questions satisfactorily. When I returned home, the employer had already called me to start working the next day. God gave me a job that changed my life. Another of my prayer requests to God was to help me find a man who would love me and my children. Right there in that place

From Darkness to Light   147

I got the two things I had asked. It was obvious that God favored me. As it often happens, when God fixed my problems I forgot about Him. For many years I lived away from God. I only remembered Him when I had problems. He always listened to me and came to my rescue with the unconditional love that only He has and knows how to give.

We need to know how to ask God about our needs. We must first believe that Jesus is God and tell Him that we recognize what He did for us on the cross of Calvary. When we sincerely seek him, His Holy Spirit approaches us convicting us of sin. At that time we sincerely repent and ask for forgiveness for our sins. He instantly justifies and sanctifies us. He removes all our sins no matter the severity of them. Our sins are the barrier that stands between us and God. The Lord's Prayer tells us that when we pray we should ask for forgiveness. The following testimony supports my point. I had a brother who lived a troubled life. I was always tormented by his lifestyle. He always looked for me to help him out of his problems. At one point I was so frustrated. I knelt on the floor and asked God for help with all my heart. I prayed to God to take my brother out of the lifestyle he was involved. The Lord gave him many opportunities to change but he never wanted to. The night when I was told that my brother was dead, I immediately remembered my request. With immense pain for the loss and great resentment against God, I dropped to my knees. I complained to God for my brother's death. I explained to Him that I wanted Him to change my brother lifestyle; I did not want him dead. I felt at that time that God told me that He does not force anyone to do what they do not want to do. We must express to God our needs and ask Him to do only His will. We do not know what really suits us, but God knows it because He already saw our lives completely. My brother went to jail three or four times accused of domestic violence before dying. The last time he left the prison; he called me and said that he had decided to change. He told me that he had already made the same promise several times and this time was not going to promise anything. He just said that his life would be different and that I was going to see that. He was murdered eight days after he came out of jail. Yes I hope to see him in the afterlife. I feel that God gave him His grace and forgiveness while he was in jail right before he died. He assured me that his life would be different and he said it in a way that sounded very convincing. He wanted to move back with his wife and asked for my opinion. I am now claiming the promise God made to His disciples. "For the promise is to you and to your children, and to all who are afar off, as many as the Lord our God will call" (Acts 2:39).

Chapter 20

The Universal Commandment

*Go therefore and make disciples of all the nations, baptizing
them in the name of the Father and of the Son and of the Holy
Spirit,*

Matthew 28:19

We can make a difference in the lives of others if we follow God's
great commission. God created us all with a purpose which must
be achieved it if we want to live peacefully. God's main business is the salvation of souls. We are like trees that He planted to give fruits for others to eat
and be satisfied. Jesus said that every fruit tree not producing fruits must be
cut and thrown to the fire using a fig tree as an example. The church of God
just as the human body needs all types of members to function properly. The
church is the body of Christ and Christ is the head (Colossians 1:18). All His
children must play a particular role in the body, the church. The functions
are assigned according to the will of God and the gifts He has given to each
one of His children. How do we know what is the purpose for which we
were called? Jesus left a great commission for all His disciples. They must go

150   Breaking Bondages

around the world making more disciples and baptizing them. When we have a relationship with God, He prepares and guides us in fulfilling that commission. He moves people from one place to another and provides them with the means to serve according to His purpose. God knows the intentions of our heart and hears the prayers of the righteous. People sometimes get desperate when do not see an immediate answer to their request. They believe He is ignoring them, but that is not true. God works at His own pace as He is building our faith and preparing us to make sure we do not fail Him.

Serving God means involvement in the salvation of souls. Rescuing souls is a difficult job that requires an in-depth training because it is required to fight like soldiers against spiritual and demonic forces. The soldiers must be well prepared and equipped with the armor of God. They cannot go to war without a sword or a weapon, which is the Word of God. Faith is the shield that will stop the fiery darts thrown by the devil (Ephesians 6:10-18). The training camps are surrounded by demons. What I mean by this is the devil is always following the soldiers of God trying to distract them. When the devil sees they are preparing to take souls away from him, he feels threatened. He sets obstacles in their way and all kinds of hindrances to discourage them. He never gives up and uses all kinds of tricks to deceive them. When he cannot stop them, he uses their closest friends and family to try to deter them and take away their peace. The following testimony illustrates how the Lord protects us from the devil. My faith grew since the moment I met the Lord due to the circumstances in which I met Him. My faith was big, but I was not armed with the sword, which is the Word of God or with the rest of the equipment. I thought I was able to confront the enemy and defeat him. The Lord knows if we are ready or not. At the beginning of our walk with God we feel all-knowing and all-powerful because we are spiritual children. Children do not understand the consequences of their actions due to their immaturity. God is watching us all the time and allows us small lessons accordingly. If we are not yet strong in faith and in the Word God He will not allow us to face the enemy directly.

God's school is the best! At His school there is neither cheating nor favoritism. Mexico is infested by all types of demons. When I went to see my brother who had just been released from a kidnapping, my heavenly Father made sure I was well protected. There were rumors that one of my relatives was possessed by demons. I wanted to approach her but my Lord Jesus Christ would not let me. Twice I walked to her house carrying my Bible but I could never approach her for one reason or another. On one occasion while talking to her niece about the dangers the family faced, a demon roared like a mad dog right next to us. The next day I tried again to approach her but I could only talk to her sister-in-law. She told me how much she feared for her brother. I learned that she had tried to kill him on several occasions. She had stabbed some scissors in his back once. I prayed with the sister-in-law for protection and we read the Bible. I explained to them about the need to be sanctified to defeat the enemy that was causing so many problems in that family. When my mom came looking for me to go back home, a weird thing happened in our way. As we approached the church which has a large cross on the roof, we perceived a strong smell of butane gas. The smell was as strong as if we inhaled it directly from an exhaust pipe. At the time we smelled the gas, I also felt goose bumps through my body. My mom who was right next to me did not feel the chills, but she asked who could be releasing gas? Now that I know a little more about the Scriptures, I understand that I was not well armed yet to face the enemy.

The Tests Get Harder

God is the best father. He watches over His children day and night to ensure they succeed in their call. He is continually testing them. He provides them with the opportunities to put into practice what they have recently learned. Through this testimony I am sharing how I was allowed to fight directly with the enemy. A violent altercation started in the car. My twenty year old son threatened to kill his younger sister for unknown reasons. I was unaware they had argued earlier. When I heard what my son said to my daughter, I raised a hand and began to pray. As my son saw me praying, he turned to me and began to threaten me. He was swearing at me with a dreadful hatred reflected in his face. I stopped my car at the closest gas station to try to resolve the problem. As soon as I stopped the car, my son got out of the back seat and rushed to open my door violently. I quickly

152   Breaking Bondages

locked my door. When he saw that he could not open it; he began to kick it shouting insults, blaspheming and asking for my Bible to destroy it. I kept praying with my hands up asking for divine help. God immediately sent the necessary help. Three men who were there came to help us until my son left. Still casting insults at us, my son got on the bus and went to school. The problem did not end there; the test became more intense when my husband was involved in the problem. Efforts to discuss and reach a settlement were all repulsed with death threats for everyone in the family. When I arrived at work, in the parking lot, God suggested to me to go back to my house to anoint it with oil. I anointed the entire house including my son's bed, clothes and shoes. I commanded the evil forces to withdraw from it. I asked God to send divine protection to take care of my home and my children. Soon he turned back to normal, to be the same affectionate boy he usually is. Three days later he brought me a gift telling me how much he loves me.

Police cannot help the demonized. My husband and I went to the police station trying to get protection because my husband did not believe what I said. On my way to the police station I was praying for my son. I asked God not to allow us to do something that would be so adverse to my child, and against God's will. The police ignored our complaints. They told us to wait until he got violent again and then call them. The text messages with threats were not enough. To get a restraining order they told us to go to the court, and for that we needed an appointment. I give thanks to the Lord for He prevented us from hurting my son more than he already was. This happened in the middle of a twenty-one day fasting period. The Lord led me in this fasting to strengthen me to pass this test. It was clear my son was under the influence of evil forces. He had allowed them into his life because of his lifestyle. A few days before, I noticed that his character was becoming aggressive. He was not talking to anyone. He spent hours making bracelets with quartz using the computer. He would make nasty comments about God to bother me. I learned that I needed to fast, although I did not know the reason. God knew it, since there are strong demons that would only go away through fasting and prayer (Mat. 17:21). The storm lasted all day but by nightfall it was over. After the storm, I began to reflect on the damage I would have caused to my poor child by sending him to prison in

The Universal Commandment   153

that deplorable state. I can imagine how hard it would be for my poor child to know that his own parents instead of helping were harming him. God does not abandon us in testing periods if we ask for help.

I was led into fasting to rescue two of my children. A week later God gave me another ordeal. My daughter came to visit me. She was walking away from God and also from me. The Lord brought her home and I was able to speak to her. For months I tried to talk to her but it was impossible. She avoided me at all costs blaming me for her problems. God had made me feel that He had a surprise for me that day. My hands were itching all day. I asked God to prepare me for that surprise. While praying, He reminded me that my daughter always makes her drama to avoid my advice because it would cramp her lifestyle. My bedroom is a place where I connect with the Lord and she came over. I told her that I did not like her attire for it looked like a Halloween costume. I proceeded wrongly and hurt her feelings. She reacted very defensively using her customized drama. I prayed in my mind as I observed her eyes. Then she began to mourn lamenting how unhappy she was. I explained that it was because she had turned away from God. She said that she had lost all her faith because God never listened to her; that she did not care for Him anymore. She went on sharing that she had done several things she knew were wrong according to God's standards. I assured her that God forgives even the darkest sins if we truly repent of having committed them. Then she challenged me, "Will you forgive me as well for all the things I have done?" She proceeded to remove her clothes to show me all her tattoos. She thought that I was not going to forgive her since she knew my views. For me that was the hardest part of the test. I had to learn to forgive.

Forgiving is impossible without God's support. The Bible sates that we are the temple of the Holy Spirit and we must keep it clean (1 Cor. 3:16). The tattoos by themselves are already disobedience to God, but her tattoos were all related with the dark world. All Halloween related creatures decorated her body. I was absolutely disappointed and disheartened because I knew that there was nothing to do. She expected to hear a series of nagging and reproaches from me, but my reaction was completely opposite. I asked her to join me in prayer to ask God for forgiveness together. I took oil to anoint her but she objected to it, complaining that it would cause acne. I anointed her feet and her back. With oil in my hands I took hers and begged God to have mercy for my daughter and grant her forgiveness. She pulled her hands away from mine and continued discussing her problems and frustrations as she cleaned the oil from her shoes. She was completely insolent and I could see the traits of Satan in her face. She was contradicting me and ignoring all my advice which alerted me to do something else. I had to rebuke those demons that were torturing her to the degree of hurting herself. She confessed that besides all the tattoos, she had to cut her body to feel pain because she needed it. I anointed my hands with oil and hugged her, then I ordered the evil spirit to stay away from her in the name of Jesus Christ and they left. When the demons left, we continued talking peacefully and ate dinner together. That night God showed me in a dream that my daughter was a baby that had fallen to the bottom of a murky pool, where she was covered by a dark colored towel. I had to look carefully among all the people who were at the bottom of the pool in order to find my girl who was about to drown. I dragged her out of the water thinking that she was already dead. I laid her face down and she started to vomit a lot of water. Moments later she began to breathe hard for she was still alive. I wrapped her with a towel, hugged her against my chest and walked onto a bus taking her with me. God showed me that my daughter was about to lose her salvation and how His mercy brought me to rescue her. When she left the house I advised her to talk to God on her way and she said that she would. God prepared me to release my children. Hallelujah!

The Enemy Does Not Sleep

And no wonder! For Satan himself transforms himself into an angel of light. Therefore it is no great thing if his ministers also transform themselves into ministers of righteousness, whose end will be according to their works.

2 Corinthians 11:14-15

The devil uses religious trickery to deceive people. Today it is common to hear people talking about miracles and wonders performed by their idols. The verse above supports their point. It was not God but the devil that performed those signs to keep them lost. God will not contradict His word. The Holy Spirit has guided me to discern right from wrong. One evening I talked to God while I watered my plants. I expressed to God my doubts and my desire to know the truth. I had been reading the Bible for several months and had not found anything telling me that Jesus' mother was the intermediary between us and the Father as I used to believe. I asked God to teach me how to pray because I did not want to offend Him, nor to Virgin Mary. Early in the morning something awoke me when the clock displayed 4:44. I got up and sat on the edge of my bed to pray. As I sat down I saw a lady approaching me. She was dressed in light clothing and a white veil covering her head. Her body was hunched over as if she was very upset. She stopped like about six feet away from me and quickly disappeared. Right after this vision I evoked that my parents used to tell us that Virgin Mary was the mediator between us and God. As soon as I recalled that Mary was the intercessor, the smiling face of a pretty lady appeared in front of me. Her round and beautiful face beckoned me by shaking her head that she actually was the mediator. That I could trust in her. She was walking towards me with her head down implying that she was sad or offended because I had doubted

156 Breaking Bondages

her lately. Then when I remembered what the Catholic religion teaches about her, she was happy. This was a hard attempt of Satan to continue deceiving me.

All my doubts cleared by reading the scriptures. I lay down thinking about the vision or appearance and could no longer sleep. I prayed and talked to God in silence so as not to wake up my husband. I asked Him if that was the answer to my question from the day before. At daybreak I opened the Bible randomly and the first thing I saw was a phrase that says praise God. I closed and I opened several times trying to get a different answer. Every time I opened it up I would read that we should only worship God. It was then that I realized that the devil was trying to make me believe that Mary the mother of Jesus is the queen of heaven and the mediator between God and Man. He wanted me to present my prayers to the wrong person so they would never reach to God. The only liaison between us and the Father is Jesus Christ. (1Tim.2: 5). Although Mary was a great woman, she was not given the title of high priest nor had she died for our sins. The Bible says that Jesus is the only one who has risen from the dead to give us salvation (I Corinthians 15:23). Even Mary the mother of Jesus called Jesus my Lord and Savior. She also needed a Savior as well as all of us do (Luke 1:47).

My former religion taught me Mary never died; that she ascended into heaven with her own body. According to the Holy Scriptures there are two people who ascended to heaven without dying; they are Enoch and the prophet Elijah. If Mary had ascended to heaven as some people believe, this would be written in the Scriptures, but there are no records of it. I am dedicating this space to her just to clarify some doubts about the way we should see her based on what it is written in the Holy Bible. She was the mother of our savior Jesus Christ and it is certainly the most blessed women of the universe (Luke 1:42). She was not only the mother of our Savior, but she was also the mother of two apostles, Judas and James (Gal 1:19). She was also the adopted mother of the Apostle John as a command of Jesus at the time of His death. She had the honor to carry in her womb the fruit of the Holy Spirit who is our Lord Jesus Christ, and as such should be admired but not praised. She had instructed the waiters at the wedding in Canaan to do all what Jesus would say. The only one who deserves all the praise and honor

The Universal Commandment 157

is God. If Mary could see how people disobey God to praise her, she would be very sad and disappointed. The Bible says in heaven there will be no more pain; thank God (Revelation 21:4). Therefore we can deduce the dead do not look at us, otherwise they would suffer much to see the things we do. Mary died like any other person and she cannot see or hear us, much less intercede for us. The story about the rich man and the beggar Lazarus tells us that the dead cannot come back to the world (Luke 16:19).

A great miracle performed by God in my family increased my faith. The kidnapping release of my brother completely changed my life. My family in Mexico was very surprised to see my transformation. They started to tease me by calling me sister as Christians usually do. The Lord Jesus Christ has never left me alone since I decided to follow Him. I have peace in my life regardless of all the skepticism and rejection. I kept reading and studying the scriptures seeking the truth. I was trying very hard to get closer to God while the devil was trying to dissuade me from the truth. One day I came back home from work and laid down to rest a little bit because I had to go back to my other job. I covered my face with my arms and tried to sleep. As soon as I closed my eyes I saw a vision. A handsome man came into my room and stood near me. His hair and beard were long; and looked like the portraits and images of Jesus in some of the churches I have visited. He stood beside me and looked at me for a moment. As I looked at him, my mind began to repeat "I love Jesus". He obviously did not like my reaction. His beautiful face began to be distorted as he opened a big mouth and soon was gone. When he left, I continued resting peacefully knowing that the Lord watches us even when we are sleeping.

Strange things happened on a trip to Mexico. I planned a short trip to visit my ill mother. My mom had pictures and statues of idols everywhere in the house. I tried to ignore the fact that they bothered me to avoid problems with my mom. It was very difficult to have peace in that place full of demons. I could clearly sense that the Guadalupe's image would make gestures trying to get my attention. God led me into fasting and Bible reading all the time I spent there. I had to carry my Bible all day long to make me feel safe. I did not show any reverence or interest in these so-called saints. I knew that those who do it are disobeying the first commandment of loving God alone.

158   Breaking Bondages

I ignored them all the way, and this is how we should ignore the devil since he does not deserve any attention. He has been defeated by Jesus through His death on the cross. It was his intention to continue making me believe in the images that were in the house and in the churches. He was trying to get me away from the commandments of God which I have learned directly from the Bible. The first commandment says that we have no other gods. *"Let us not do any type of images to worship them because God is strong and jealous, visiting the iniquity of the fathers upon the children unto the third and fourth generation of those who disobey. It also says it is showing mercy to thousands, to those who love Him and keep His commandments"* (Exodus 20:3-6).

Idolatry is the root of many sins

...because, although they knew God, they did not glorify Him as God, nor were thankful, but became futile in their thoughts, and their foolish hearts were darkened. Professing to be wise, they became fools, and changed the glory of the incorruptible God into an image made like corruptible man— and birds and four-footed animals and creeping things. Therefore God also gave them up to uncleanness, in the lusts of their hearts, to dishonor their bodies among themselves,

Romans 1:21-24

Many questions can be answered by reading the above passage. People often say God is unfair for all the bad things that happen in their lives. It is not God who causes the problems but our idolatry. Man refuses to follow God and makes his own gods and worships them. From the beginning of time, men's disobedience alienated them from God which allowed them to

The Universal Commandment   159

follow their reprobate minds thus incurring in all kinds of sins. Homosexuality, lesbianism and all the sins of the flesh are the result of worshiping other gods and images. Malignant tumors can also be a consequence of idolatry. The Philistines stole the Ark of the Covenant where God's glory dwelt and put it in the temple of one of their gods. The scriptures tell that the next day in the morning when they went to visit their temple, they found the statue of Dagon their god face down on the ground before the Ark of the Lord. They put him back in his altar and left. The next day he was found again on the ground but this time there was just part of his body because his head and hands were lying on the threshold. The wrath of the Lord brought devastation to the people who were afflicted with tumors. Thousands of people were killed for trying to put God next to their idol (1 Samuel 5:1-12). God was very precise in His instructions. In the Ten Commandments He states that no other gods are allowed because He is very jealous. We say that we love Him but we have our houses and our churches full of idols. God is just like a jealous husband who finds his wife with another man in his own house. He does not share His glory with anyone. He leaves us alone so we can do what it pleases us. He knows that our choices will cause pain and afflictions that would make us realize that only He can help us. He is always waiting for us to change our mind and seek him.

Chapter 21

Religious Spirits

Then all the men who knew that their wives had burned incense to other gods, with all the women who stood by, a great multitude, and all the people who dwelt in the land of Egypt, in Pathros, answered Jeremiah, saying: "As for the word that you have spoken to us in the name of the Lord, we will not listen to you! But we will certainly do whatever has gone out of our own mouth, to burn incense to the queen of heaven and pour out drink offerings to her, as we have done, we and our fathers, our kings and our princes, in the cities of Judah and in the streets of Jerusalem. For then we had plenty of food, were well-off, and saw no trouble.

Jeremiah 44:15-17

God forbids us to worship the deceiver spirit called queen of heaven. The deceiving spirits in the world have multiplied. There is demonic spirits behind every religion in the world. The queen of heaven is one of the worst to defeat. The above passage states that the queen of heaven has been

162   Breaking Bondages

worshipped for generations. It also implies that it is a spirit that brings them physical prosperity and delusion. When people have everything they need here in earth seldom look to The Lord for help. The above passage was written hundreds of years before Mary was born; therefore, the queen cannot be Mary the mother of Jesus as many people believe. The prophet Jeremiah gave God's people a message to prevent them from the harm they were causing themselves by worshipping the queen of heaven. The rebellion of the past is present in our days. People refuse to hear the warnings against worshipping idols. There have been several women throughout history who have been worshiped by the people of their time. The title of "Queen of Heaven" has been given to women such as: Semiramis the wife and mother of Nimrod. It is believed that she cheated on her husband with her own son and had a son named Tammuz. The Chaldeans called Semiramis the wife and mother of the sun god and made an image of them to worship it. The same kind of image of a woman with a child is currently adored or worshiped by millions of Catholics in the world. The Canaanites worshiped Ashtoreth the goddess of fertility. Later the Greeks worshiped the goddess Astarte represented by the moon. Others were Inanna or Ishtar, the Sumerian goddess of fertility, which literally means "Queen of Heaven" and Diana which is mentioned in the Bible (Acts 19:35). When one disappeared there was always another that would replace it. Catholics today call "the queen of heaven" to Mary the mother of Jesus. The scriptures never call her that and they warn us against its worship (Jeremiah 7:18). If there is no other document or book inspired by the Holy Spirit where did they get this information? What are the bases for that proclamation? These questions should be asked by every Catholic to learn why they venerate Mary and other images.

You search the Scriptures, for in them you think you have eternal life; and these are they which testify of Me. But you are not willing to come to Me that you may have life.

John 5:39-40

All the doctrines are made by man and they all have some truth if they are based on the Holy Bible. We read in the passage above that eternal life depends on our closeness to Jesus, not in how much we read the Bible. Without Him, people interpret the Bible guided by their own understanding. The different interpretations have created a myriad of wrong religions. The devil can lead people astray with the Bible or without it. There are many doctrines that differ from Christianity which claim that God spoke to a prophet among their people. They are assured God gave them information to write their own book as in the case of the Mormons and Muslims. This is not to say they are right, but they at least can say they read it instead of saying I heard that in my church. There is only one truth and that is Jesus Christ. The Mormons have a book called the Book of Mormon. Followers call that book as the most sacred book of the universe. They insist Jesus came to America to preach another gospel. The apostle Paul pronounces a curse on those who preach a different gospel from what the apostles preached. (Galatians 1:6-9). For their part, Muslims were also deceived by a supposed prophet named Muhammad. They also have a book that contradicts the Gospel of Jesus Christ called the Koran. Each doctrine no matter how near or far they are from the truth is manipulated by seducing spirits. They influence the most vulnerable leaders and use them to keep people away from God. We must pray to God our Father to enlighten the minds of the people so they may find the truth and can be saved.

Angels and demons

The thief does not come except to steal, and to kill, and to destroy. I have come that they may have life, and that they may have it more abundantly.
John 10:10

The soldiers of the Lord move around fighting with the enemy. On my trip to Mexico to help my mom get the ticket to heaven I was a victim of direct attacks of the enemy. The devil is a thief that through flattery deceives its victims and steals their soul. He tried to kill me but God protected me. God has promised to be by our side. He is so powerful that the same devil

164   Breaking Bondages

trembles when he hears his name. Satan does not have power to give or to take away life. I am not saying that we should underestimate him. What I am saying is that we can win every battle if we have Jesus Christ as our ally. The devil never gives up. When we resist him he flies away from us to mess around with our family and closest friends. He alters our relationships by putting wrong ideas in their minds. All of a sudden we receive false accusations that take away our peace. They call us judgmental because we disagree with the ways of the world. We feel persecuted by our own parents, brothers, husbands, wives, etc. The churches are not the exception. If we try to work harder for the Lord the disagreements arouse. The devil causes division and weakens the congregation when the leaders do not consecrate their life to the Lord. People call us radicals and rare for trying to please Christ. The Bible says that spiritual things are foolishness to those who live according to the flesh (I Corinthians 2:14).

The spirits' manifestations lead us to God although we hardly see it that way. My oldest son out of anger told me that he hated my God. I ordered him to go to sleep early because he had to go to school the next day. He had a tantrum and said he would stay up in the garage until he was tired. I sensed something ugly was going to happen and begged him not to go to the garage. He finally listened to me and went to his bed. As soon as I lay down I felt when something gently fell near my feet on the bed. I thought it was our cat and waited for her to walk up to my pillow. Indeed what fell into my bed walked towards my pillow and gently shook it trying to get my attention. I sat up to see what was it and saw nothing. The cat was not there and my husband who was in the same bed did not sense anything. A few seconds later we heard a loud scream coming from my son's bedroom. He asked me to bring the oil to anoint him. He was being tormented by a strong force that did not allow him to move. My husband and I ran to his room where we found him trembling with fear. We could also feel a cold sensation, which gave us goose bumps. We prayed rebuking the demon in Jesus' name and soon things went back to normal. The Lord sent an angel to presage us that something bad was happening to my son. This test showed my children that we need to obey God's commandments and obey our parents as well. My children often feel strange forces near them but are no longer afraid. They know the demons

Religious Spirits   165

cannot do anything while they are protected by our Lord Jesus Christ.

The devil uses the closest members of our family to take away our peace. My youngest son has been used by the devil to try to harm and destroy our family a few times. The first time we had a Bible study at home my son became irrational. The fight was awful; his face looked dark and disfigured. The enemy obviously disagreed with the decision to study the word of God in its former domain. While my two sons were arguing and fighting I prayed with some members of the group until the storm calmed down. After the storm had passed, my son came to me very sad. He expressed that he was ashamed of having felt a desire to kill his father and brother. I hugged him and told him not to worry because God would never allow it. My husband and my children belong to God based on His promises. The promise is for God's children and I am His daughter (Acts 2:39). He adopted me when I repented of my sins and was baptized. Satan also wanted to thwart the second meeting. Two hours before the second Bible study, I was told that my youngest daughter's body was covered with red rashes that had appeared suddenly. My husband suggested that we cancel the meeting that night. I pondered it, but at the moment I felt that we should have it. I recommended to my husband that we should proceed with the plans even if we had to go to the emergency room later. At ten p.m. we took our daughter to the hospital where she underwent tests to determine the problem. They did some tests but did not find any allergic reaction to anything. The rashes disappeared unexpectedly the same way they appeared. This was obviously a strategy of the devil to stop the plans of God for our family. Now I know that God protects us from all these attacks to accomplish His plans. Every day I ask our Lord Jesus to protect my family and I move around trying to serve Him. I leave all my battles in God's hands for I know He will fight them and I do not have to worry.

The devil cannot touch our heart. He has only one way to come into our lives and that window is the mind. He uses every possible channel and all circumstances. When he penetrates into our mind it begins to confuse us with negative thoughts. I previously mentioned that on more than two occasions clearly felt a terrible force entering my brain while I slept. Everything disappeared from my mind and I could only see darkness. I felt a huge energy that span my brain rapidly while a voice in me kept repeating "I love Jesus Christ." After several attempts to combat, he left me alone because he could not stand to hear me say that I love Jesus Christ. The spirit of God within me fought the enemy and did not let him to possess my mind. The Holy Spirit is always alert to defend us against the evil one. The devil does not always try to force us like in my case. Most of the time, he does things in a subtle way. He conveys us that it is impossible to please God. He tries very hard to humiliate us so we can lose heart. Our relationship with God will determine the way we will accomplish our call. Jesus said his sheep will follow him (John 10: 27-30). When the devil sees that he has lost souls, he despairs and tries by all means to bring us back. The assaults become worse because he is always looking for our weaknesses. If he knows we are weak to the opposite sex, he places the temptation on our path to make us fall. If he knows we are ambitious for money, fame or glory, he presents us opportunities to achieve them. Having money is not bad if we can use it to serve the Lord. The problem is that while we are so busy earning it, we walk away from the things of God. No man can serve two masters at the same time; we either love God or love money (Matthew 6:24). To succeed in this battle against the forces of darkness, we need to trust God and let Him guide us. We must remind the devil that He who is in us is strong and powerful. God promised to protect us always and He will always keep His promises (1 John 4:4).

Chapter 22

Spiritual Gifts and its Mistakes

There are diversities of gifts, but the same Spirit. There are differences of ministries, but the same Lord. And there are diversities of activities, but it is the same God who works all in all. But the manifestation of the Spirit is given to each one for the profit of all: for to one is given the word of wisdom through the Spirit, to another the word of knowledge through the same Spirit, to another faith by the same Spirit, to another gifts of healings by the same Spirit, to another the working of miracles, to another prophecy, to another discerning of spirits, to another different kinds of tongues, to another the interpretation of tongues. But one and the same Spirit works all these things, distributing to each one individually as He wills.

1 Cor. 12:4-11

We cannot serve the Lord if we are not equipped to do so. To be prepared to serve means to be baptized with the Holy Spirit. Peter explained to the people present at the coming of the Holy Spirit that Jesus was the Lord. He told them that to receive Him they needed to repent and

168   Breaking Bondages

be baptized in His name. The Holy Spirit transforms our lives and equips us with gifts to succeed in our call. Yes we all are called to do great things for the Lord. The Holy Spirit grants the gifts to us according to His will and we are not to question it. The gift of discernment would help us to distinguish God's voice and follow Him in obedience. He will always be with us to guide us step by step in our new life. He will provide us with opportunities to use our gifts or abilities in different situations. He will connect us with people who can teach us new strategies to fight our future battles. As we start growing, The Lord increases our duties and leads us to seek wisdom from above. The Lord has a purpose for each of us and He will make it clear in due time. We are all called to serve in one or more of the five ministries He established. At the beginning of my journey with God I was told by an acquaintance of a friend that I needed to speak in tongues in order to communicate with The Lord. I was very naive and believed her. Then I concluded that I would need someone to pray for my needs because I did not have that gift. I was calling her very often to pray for my needs which were many. She would always pray in a language that I did not understand but she was really repeating the same utterances. While doing that kind of communication if we can call it that, she said that she was having direct communication with the Lord. She was translating simultaneously what the Lord was responding to my prayers. I was very excited and wanted to talk to her often although the calls were expensive. We talked for hours because I thought she was very close to the Lord and I wanted to be like her.

1 Corinthians chapter 12 makes it clear that each Christian is given spiritual gifts according to the Holy Spirit's will. But since I did not know better I made a list of requests to God including the gift of tongues. I wanted to talk to Him directly as the lady made me believe. Such was my ignorance that one day I decided to imitate her by repeating the same utterances which I memorized. My husband advised me against doing such absurdity. He told me that by doing that I could be speaking directly to the devil. I ignored him and kept repeating what I learned from that lady until the Lord spoke to me. I heard clearly the voice of the Holy Spirit telling me not to do that. God was confirming to me what my husband had said and I finally stopped. I was led to read the Holy Scriptures where I have learned that God gives us the gifts

Spiritual Gifts and its Mistakes   169

we need to accomplish our call. Furthermore, the apostle Paul recommends that we ask God preferably for the gifts that will build up the church such as the gift of prophecy and exhortation. We all can communicate with God through our Lord Jesus Christ who is our mediator. God understands our own language. All we need to ask for is that He equips and transforms us in order to serve Him. Some erroneous doctrines teach that the gift of tongues is the only sign that we were baptized by the Holy Spirit but the Bible does not say that. This gift is only a sign but there are other gifts that serve as signals as well. They all come from the same Spirit. Because of such doctrines many people pretend to speak in tongues when they in reality do not possess the gift. I,myself, used to pretend to speak in tongues because I thought it would connect me to The Lord. The desire to experience God's presence makes us fall into the deception of the enemy. Some others want people to think they are more spiritual and we heard them repeating the same words publicly. We must be careful that everything we do builds upon the church and does not become a stumbling block. The angelic tongues serve to edify the person therefore; the one who has this gift should use it in private when talking to God. The apostle Paul advises us not to use it in public if there is no one to interpret it. The interpretation of tongues is another gift of the Holy Spirit (1 Corinthians 14:12-13).

Spiritual manifestations

The Lord exhorts us to move up. A person while praying prophesied about my life. She said several things that I did not understand because I did not know the Lord. Among the things she said was that God was going to move me up to another level. That my life was going to be totally different. I thought I was going to be promoted at work but I never imagined how my life would change drastically at my age. This was unbelievable but truthful. My life now is completely different from the life I had before. I was born again thanks to the trials I passed which opened my eyes to seek God. As a new creature, I am not interested in all the parties I used to enjoy. My greatest desire now is to know more intimately our heavenly Father. The day before I was baptized I prayed and worshipped for a while expressing to God how happy I was to do His will. I wanted to see in my baptism something like what happened when Jesus was baptized. In my ignorance I expected to see a dove descending from heaven to pose on my shoulder. I wanted to listen to the heavenly Father telling me publicly that I was His beloved daughter. After praying for a while, I randomly opened the Bible to read something. Upon opening it, a verse caught my attention. "From this day on you shall call me Father (Jer. 3:4). I clearly felt that He was talking to me as I was filled with an unexplained joy. I was adopted as His daughter in advance to my baptism to reward my obedience. My adoption came privately but with power. I am very proud to have the Creator of the universe as my Father. The Lord spoke to me using the Bible to exhort me to continue living in obedience to His ordinances.

The evil has been increased in the world

For we do not wrestle against flesh and blood, but against principalities, against powers, against the rulers of the darkness of this age, against spiritual hosts of wickedness in the heavenly places.

Ephesians 6:12

All those who have decided to serve God must face spiritual warfare. For some the spiritual battles are more intense than for others, but no one escapes them. The intensity of the fights depends on our efforts to recover souls for God. Throughout the scriptures we see descriptions of evil forces that influence the mind and behavior of people. The Christian church has faced fiery battles from its origin. Prophets, apostles, evangelist and missionaries have been murdered for the sake of the Gospel of Jesus Christ. In our present time, the missionaries have tremendous challenges to face in order to expand the kingdom. Christians are persecuted by the government, the

Spiritual Gifts and its Mistakes   171

pagan religions, and even by the same so-called Christian doctrines. Today the religious spirits have multiplied and have invaded Christian churches. In most churches we see pastors and leaders who are governed by man-made dogmas and their structures. To follow the dogmas of their religion they compromise their relationship with God and the salvation of the sheep. They want to please God and the world at the same time although the Holy Scriptures inform us that it cannot be possible (James 4:2–6). The Jewish priests and the Jerusalem authorities forbade the apostles to teach about Jesus. But they continued to do so to give us an example to follow as stated in the following quote "But Peter and the *other* apostles answered and said: "We ought to obey God rather than men" (Acts 5:29).

The apostasy has increased considerably which indicates the return our Lord Jesus Christ is nearer. The Christian churches are following the schemes of the devil which are dragging them downward. The churches of God are now dens of thieves and liars who seek their own benefit thus deceiving the immature followers. It seems as if we are seeing "the abomination that causes desolation" mentioned in the book of Daniel and in Matthew (Daniel 12:11 and Matthew 24:15). We see our children and youth lost due to various evils that are dragging them hopelessly to the abyss. The sexual immorality, wickedness, corruption, crime, divorce and corrupt churches have increased on a large scale. Needless to say, behind all these problems are the forces of evil. Homosexuality is viewed as a sociological problem caused by the environment and by some genetically alterations. God is accused of being capricious and spiteful for not approving these misconducts. What people ignore is that all evils are the result of our disobedience and it was caused by the devil.

Spiritual warfare can be defined as any confrontation against the forces of darkness. The apostle Peter warns us to stay alert. Our adversary the devil is always lurking like a roaring lion ready to devour its prey (1 Peter 5:8-9). To resist the enemy we must stand firm in our faith in God our savior. The Holy Scriptures equip us with weapons to fight the evil. The Word of God is the sword to fight against the devil. Jesus conquered the evil one when He died on the cross at Calvary (Col. 2: 15). Through suffering, we like Jesus, will be conquerors as well. Our life of prayers and sacrifice will bring salvation for

172   Breaking Bondages

our relatives and friends. The devil needs to be reminded that our Father has prepared a burning pit for him where he will be locked up for eternity. To face the enemy we must remain in constant prayer and perfect obedience to God our Father. We must be dressed with the full armor of God (Ephesians 6:10-18). That armor is available to all who want to use it.

> *...being filled with all unrighteousness, sexual immorality,[a] wickedness, covetousness, maliciousness; full of envy, murder, strife, deceit, evil-mindedness; they are whisperers, backbiters, haters of God, violent, proud, boasters, inventors of evil things, disobedient to parents, undiscerning, untrustworthy, unloving, unforgiving, unmerciful;*
>
> *Romans 1:29-31*

This passage is a mirror of what we see in the world today. Everyone from small children to adults are affected by the forces of darkness in many ways to a point of total spiritual desolation. Schools are being invaded by all the spirits of evil, which are destroying the future of the world, our children. The schools are dens of perversion. Children ten years and older are using drugs and alcohol, which are becoming more and more accessible. Sex and pornography also abound in educational fields through all the technology available to them. They are not interested in learning academic subjects. The students' minds are dominated by addictions and they will do whatever it takes to get drugs. Young people have no respect for themselves or anyone else. Then we see the desperate parents seeking for help in the secular world. They are trying to find solution to their problems in the wrong place. Schools and government institutions offer certain programs, which ultimately are not the solution. In the parents meetings they sadly report their efforts trying to find the assistance for their children. They go through counseling sessions with psychologists and psychiatrists but their children have gotten worse instead of better. They enroll their children in educational and sports

Spiritual Gifts and its Mistakes   173

programs but the problem continues. The only one that can help them is God but they reject Him. The darkness in which they live prevents them from seeing the truth. God is offering solutions to the problems of the schools but people do not see them. Christian clubs exist in most schools but only a few students take advantage of them. I speak to parents about the Christian club at school and most of them reject it. Other parents let their children decide whether or not to attend. The children are easily influenced by their peers who convince them to stay away from God. The problems will not be solved until the parents decide to walk in the light, which is Jesus Christ.

The demons still possess people now as in the time when Jesus lived on earth. The demon possessed individual displays strength way superior of that of any strong man. The girl, I mentioned in a former chapter could not be restrained by four men. She would easily push them away to continue harming herself or trying to harm others. The Gadarene man is a biblical example of this sort. He would forcefully break strong chains to loosen himself and be able to do what the demons wanted him to do (Luke 8:27). When I was studying at the seminary, a pastor shared with us an experience with a demonized person. During a meeting, a young girl was behaving very strange. The whole time she was making gestures and moving compulsively. The pastor was concerned and offered to help her if she needed it. She did not respond, looked at him, wrinkled her nose and turned to the other way. Other people in the group also tried to talk to her but she just growled at them in a low and husky voice. The group began to pray for her. Upset at their prayers, she bent down and crawled under a table. The pastor asked three of the strongest guys to help her out from under the table. They removed her without much difficulty for she was very thin. As they sat her down, with a supernatural force pushed them all to the floor. Then she went back and sat under the table staring and growling with her gravelly voice. It took them days of fasting and praying to release this girl from the demon that was imprisoning her. I learned from this that God provides us with opportunities to grow spiritually if that is what we want.

We all are God's creation. Only the people who believe in Jesus and obey Him are children of God. They become His children from the time they are baptized with the Holy Spirit (Acts 1:5, Acts 11:16). When we are adopted as

174   Breaking Bondages

children of God, we become enemies with the devil. To overcome him, we must recognize two things: Our identity and the identity of the world. The world is led by the devil and we must be alert praying to avoid following its stratagems. The devil gains influence through its lying spirits. They hide the truth which prevents people from recognizing right from wrong. Confused and deceived by the devil, people surrender to the pleasures of the world. They fall into sinful habits such as greed, arrogance, laziness, envy, selfishness, violence, hunger for power, crime, fornication, drugs, etc. The demonic spirits also make great confusion in secular groups. They use systems such as financial, political and social institutions to turn people away from God. These institutions offer people comfortable ways of living where people do not see the need for a savior. People gain a new identity when they are associated with Jesus Christ. They become citizens of the kingdom of God and heirs of Jesus. They do not belong to this world although they still live in it. They are new creatures or children of the Most High and have power to overcome the attacks of the devil. All who receive Jesus in their hearts and believe in him, God gave them the right to be called His children (John 1:12). God has given them the power to fight the forces of evil wherever they go and the devil knows who they are.

The devil does not bother us, until we get near to God. Our spiritual warfare increases when we imitate Jesus with our lifestyle. The devil tempts us with the things we like the most. The temptations become more attractive for new creatures. The darts that the devil throws follow us everywhere but we are not alone. The Holy Spirit is with us to protect and defend from all the temptations. God sends His divine protection to look after us and protect us as we move from spiritual babies to mature Christians. In this process we can be deceived by evil spirits as in the case of the apostle Peter but Jesus rebukes the devil. Jesus spoke boldly to the demon: *"But He turned and said to Peter, 'Get behind Me, Satan! You are an offense to Me, for you are not mindful of the things of God, but the things of men.'"*(Matthew 16:23). Christians are involved in spiritual warfare every day and have to make an important decision. They can choose between fighting and win those battles with the help of God, or give up. If we decide to stand aside we not only are losing our souls but also those of the people our Lord has made us responsible for. However, we must be very cunning to declare war on the enemy. To do this we must pray ceaselessly, read the Bible, obey God in everything, fast, and ask others to pray for our protection. We should not fear the devil but we have to take the dispute seriously. Before engaging in spiritual warfare we must know the schemes of the devil or the way he works. We must pray for wisdom and discernment to identify the enemy and to understand that we are not dealing with flesh and blood but against powers and principalities. When we fight with the spirits instead of people, our human relations return to normal. The apostle Paul recommended that we keep well placed the armor of God and pray every day, without ceasing to be prepared for the bad days. Although the war is long and hard, the victory is secured as long as we trust in God for He is indeed who fights our battles.

Chapter 23

Selfishness and Its Consequences

Therefore, to him who knows to do good and does not do it, to him it is sin.

James 4:17

The person who knows the difference between right and wrong and chooses to do evil is committing sin. The concept of sin in the Bible is found directly from the tragic event in the Garden of Eden. Cain and Abel are the first victims for the disobedience of their parents. The serpent told Eve that if she ate the forbidden fruit their eyes were going to be opened and that they would be just like God. The effect was totally the opposite. By disobeying the commandment of God, Adam and Eve were transferred from light to darkness. Their children were born with selfishness and other negative trends. Cain was not giving the best of his harvest to God for he was selfish. The Lord warned Cain about the sin he was committing and tried to convince him to change his attitude. Cain chose to ignore the warnings from God and murdered his brother Abel. As a result of his terrible sin, Cain wandered the world suffering away from God and from his family (Gen. 4:1-14). Disobedience to God and all unrighteousness is sin (1 John 5:17). We can be condemned by doubting God's Word and for lack of faith (John 3:18).

The following points will help us better understand the consequences of disobedience to God using the specific example of Cain and Abel.

Selfishness brings bitterness

+ God did not approved the selfishness of Cain and neither would He approve ours.
+ Cain lost control of his temper and became angry.
+ God tried to help, but Cain did not listen because his mind was blurred by his selfishness
+ Cain's bitterness caused him to argue with God
+ Cain's stubbornness caused him to kill his brother.

Effects of selfishness

+ Abel's blood demands punishment on earth
+ The earth does not produce enough fruit for Cain
+ Cain became a wanderer on the earth

Selfishness pulls us away from God

You yourselves bear me witness, that I said, 'I am not the Christ,' but, 'I have been sent before Him.' He who has the bride is the bridegroom; but the friend of the bridegroom, who stands and hears him, rejoices greatly because of the bridegroom's voice. Therefore this joy of mine is fulfilled.

John 3:28-29

Selfishness and Its Consequences   179

Selfishness is the root of many of our sinful acts. The Bible stresses the need to get rid of selfishness in order to grow in the eyes of God. Our human traits must be hidden to display our godly ones. John the Baptist was seeking to decrease so that Jesus could grow up. Let's see what Jesus said of him in the following biblical quote. *"Assuredly, I say to you, among those born of women there has not risen one greater than John the Baptist; but he who is least in the kingdom of heaven is greater than he"* (Matthew 11:11). Unfortunately selfishness is a negative feeling that manifests in most people including children. We hurt, rob, mistreat and disobey because we only think in our wellbeing and not about the one of others. Selfishness and love are two opposite words. Selfishness hurts and destroys, while love serves as an antidote to cure the evil of selfishness. There is a famous phrase that says, "Love is only satisfied when the loved person is happy." Love is the greatest of all the God given gifts. Love is the only thing that can revert the effects of sin in the world. Jesus commanded us to love one another, as He loved us (John 13:34). In other words God is asking us to be like Him who is all love. Let's dare it.

Free will

Finally, brethren, whatever things are true, whatever things are noble, whatever things are just, whatever things are pure, whatever things are lovely, whatever things are of good report, if there is any virtue and if there is anything praiseworthy—meditate on these things.

Philippians 4:8

God by His infinite love could not deny us anything He owns. The lack of selfishness in His purity led Him to provide us with the right to choose even though He knew the consequences. Life or death depends on the choices we make. If we choose evil we will face eternal condemnation, but if we choose righteousness we will have eternal life. Seek Christ and He will lead

180   Breaking Bondages

you to choose right from wrong. The grace and forgiveness of God changes everything. God has given us free will, which is a powerful weapon that needs to be used with divine wisdom. When we use it properly, our lives are transformed positively. When we choose to follow Christ instead of anguish and distress we have peace, joy and a great reward in heaven. The choice we have made would not only determine our quality of life but also the one of the people who depend on us. Because of our sinful nature we tend to follow the desires of the flesh and make tremendous mistakes. Our minds lead us to envy others and criticize them. Our mistakes become bondages for us and for our children. The apostle Paul exhorted the Philippians to change their way of thinking as we can see in the above quote. That exhortation is for each of us as well, for all who want to please God. Like Paul we must choose to do well and obey God.

Chapter 24

Prayer and Faith

And the apostles said to the Lord, "Increase our faith."
So the Lord said, "If you have faith as a mustard seed,
you can say to this mulberry tree, 'Be pulled up by the
roots and be planted in the sea,' and it would obey you.

Luke 17:5-6

Our prayers with faith greatly benefit us and others. Praying is only effective when people have faith that something will happen. God is moved by the believer's faith, not by their problems, or by their needs. Miracles occur according to the faith we have in what we ask. The Bible is full of examples of faith that we should imitate. The prophet Elijah was a man who had great faith. According to the Holy Scriptures we learn that in Israel it did not rain for more than three and half years because of Elijah's faith. The economic situation was very critical, people and animals perished for lack of food and water. No one prayed for changes; they just gave up for they had no faith. The prophet Elijah got tired of the drought and so he said to Ahab, "Go up, eat and drink for a big rain is coming." The Scriptures say

182 Breaking Bondages

that Elijah had a servant whom he sent to see if there were indications of rain near the ocean. "Go and look toward the sea, he ordered his servant". The servant went to look returning with negative reports. "I do not see anything." Elijah said that based solely on his faith because in the sky there was not a cloud to indicate a chance of rain. (1Kings18: 43). Just as Elijah did despite not seeing any sign of rain, he continued to pray, we should also pray for our needs no matter how big they are. We should not give up hope to win our children and the rest of the family for God. We must continue praying for them with faith that the Lord is going to turn their hearts to Him. He will change their character and even their lifestyle. If we settle for what we have the Lord is not going to make any changes. We must get on our knees and beg the Lord to change our problems into blessings. Guided by his faith Elijah commanded the servant to look again into the sea. Finally the servant reported that on the horizon appeared a little cloud which soon brought the long-awaited rain. Just as Elijah did, we must stay ever vigilant and never give up on our faith.

To have faith means to believe in the unseen, the substance of hope (Hebrews 11:1, 6). We communicate with God through prayer with faith. Prayer is a code to communicate with God translated into all the languages of the world. Faith gives us conviction our prayers will be answered but it is hard to possess it. Jesus speaks of man's frailty when he says: *"I tell you that He will avenge them speedily. Nevertheless, when the Son of Man comes, will He really find faith on the earth?"* (Luke 18:8). The Bible has several examples where the faith of people brought all sorts of benefits. Abraham before climbing to the mountain where it is believed he would sacrifice his own son, he tells the servant that he and his son were departing to worship God on the mountain and would return together. He never lost his faith and when he was about to give the deathblow to his son, God sends a ram for the burnt offering thus Isaac is rescued. He had faith that God would bring them back together and God did not fail him, nor will He forsake us if we have faith. Another striking example is that of the woman who had a flow of blood. The illness tormented her for more than twelve years. She consumed all her resources without success. Her health worsened every day but her faith grew tremendously. Fortified by this great faith she had, dared to mingle with the crowd to get to Jesus. She came up behind Jesus and touched the edge of His mantle. She knew it was enough to be cured. As a result of her act of faith, she was immediately healed of her affliction. Another example is that of the centurion who asks Jesus to heal one of his employees. Jesus agrees to go to the sick person but the centurion tells Him that He does not need to go there. This kind of faith greatly surprised Jesus. He stated that He had not seen such faith. The centurion employee was healed by Jesus remotely.

Our faith can work wonders. I have applied these testimonies to my life and the Lord has proved true to His word. The Lord is bringing huge changes to my life and ministry. After a lot of hardships, much prayer and fasting, my husband turned his life to Jesus. Now we are together serving the Lord in any mission He commands of us. I wished to start a church with people willing to serve God with all their heart. I wanted to see a reproduction of the early church illustrated in the book Acts. I prayed for over a year asking my Heavenly Father to send workers to begin that church. Right after returning from a mission trip, while listening to a pastor I sensed the Lord was telling me to dig a trench because a shower of blessings was coming. From that day on I began to pray for the rain of blessings. I communicated the idea to my brothers in Christ to pray together. The Lord began to send His fitted workers and now we are a small congregation of living stones whose sole purpose is to please God. We meet weekly to worship God and study His Word. We guide a Christian club in my workplace and we are delivering the last invitations to the wedding of the Lamb of God. Our mission field is in town visiting hospitals, convalescent homes, cemeteries and homeless shelters to bring physical and spiritual food to the poor and needed. Lately The Lord is sending us to Latin America where the need is as great as it is here. Glory be to God.

Conclusion

Our sorrows urge us to seek for spiritual help. Trials and tribulations soften our hearts to hear God' voice. We must learn to accept the pain to grow spiritually through it. Success in life is not to avoid or escape the pain, but to recognize that it was necessary to suffer in order to mature. Pain is the price you pay to enjoy something you really want to have. The best example we have comes from our Lord Jesus Christ. God loves us so much that He gave his own life in exchange for having us near Him. Suffering brings with it many benefits. What we suffer in this world is temporary and it makes us much more sensitive to the needs of others. The greatest benefit of this suffering is that it prepares us to live eternally in the presence of God.

I pray that these testimonies will lead you to recognize your need to be closer to God. Life in this world is not a destination; it is just a starting point. It is a place of mixed emotions and the prelude to an upcoming event. It is where you will get the tickets for an unimaginable and wonderful appointment for the followers of Christ. It is also the gateway to a dreadful place of torment for those who rejected Him. Our existence on this planet is a school that offers only two careers that will lead us to our final destination. If we follow Christ we are on the right path that leads to heaven and eternal life with our Creator. If we follow man and the man-made religions then we are on the wrong path, which leads to the lake of fire and brimstone better known as hell. Jesus said I am the way, the truth and the life, no one comes to the Father except through me. There is no other name given among men by which we must be saved (John 14:6, Acts 4:12).

186   Breaking Bondages

Jesus is the Word and He says: "For God so loved the world that He gave His only begotten Son, that whoever believes in Him should not perish but have everlasting life"; "The thief does not come except to steal, and to kill, and to destroy. I have come that they may have life, and that they may have *it* more abundantly" (John 3:16; 10:10). I just want to remind you that the Lord is knocking on your door at this time. Open your heart and begin to experience here on earth the peace and joy that comes from trusting in the Lord Jesus Christ. He said that in the world we would have tribulation but He left us His peace. We can have peace regardless of adverse situations if we believe and trust in the Lord blindly. The choice is ours! I am going to leave you with a poem that summarizes the Gospel.

Because He Loves You

By: Maria Eriksson

In the Scriptures we read what a prophet had said
If not for his mercy we all would be dead
His love towards us delays his return
Giving us more time, expecting us to learn

Forever, forever he is going to love you
Enduring patiently to see what you do
The years have passed and the centuries too
But He is still waiting because He loves you

As Sodom and Gomorrah we should be by now
But His enduring mercy has saved us somehow
Suffering for us His wrath has delayed
Desiring to see us in his kingdom one day

His awaited return, the apostles had preached
Spreading the news Jesus came to teach
But tired of waiting they all went to sleep
Without seeing the fruits their efforts had reaped

The teacher of mercy, the teacher of love
Showing us His feelings by sending a dove
During the baptism of Jesus by John
He opens the heavens to show us his son

Forever, forever he is going to love you
Enduring and patiently to see what you do
The years have passed and the centuries too
But He is still waiting because He loves you

May the Lord Jesus bless you always.